MARKETING YOUR JOB TALENTS

MARKETING YOUR JOB TALENTS

A Guide to Landing the Job You Want

By Shedrick McKenzie

Published by
MIDNIGHT EXPRESS BOOKS

MARKETING YOUR JOB TALENTS

Published by
MIDNIGHT EXPRESS BOOKS
POBox 69
Berryville AR 72616
(870) 210-3772
MEBooks1@yahoo.com

MARKETING YOUR JOB TALENTS

By Shedrick McKenzie

TABLE OF CONTENTS

INTRODUCTION

You want a job. And you feel that somewhere, some employer has precisely the job you want--one that fully uses your knowledge and abilities and provide challenge and opportunities for advancement. To get that job you must market your talents by showing employers the skills needed. You have a brand to sell, "you"--your knowledge, skills, and experience. Identifying and marketing your brand is an essential core competency for managing and sustaining a successful career. Empower yourself by knowing what you have to offer, what you want and how to ask for it. Your ability to market your talents, accomplishments and value within your profession, industry, and community are a key part of enhancing your brand. The demands we face today include unpredictable economy, very competitive and specialized marketplace, globalization, changing demographics, and strong leadership skills by all levels. Whether you are just out of high school, college or just looking for a fresh start, some of the techniques presented in this book will help you. It offers suggestions on how to:

- ❖ Searching for the job you're qualified for

- ❖ Writing an effective resume and cover letter

- ❖ How to be successful at interviewing for a job

This book will also cover tips on testing taking and freelancing your talents into your own small business.

In order to be successful, it is critical to set yourself apart.

Chapter 1

SELF-APPRAISAL

· ·

In This Chapter You Will Learn

➢ The definition of values, interests, and aptitudes.

➢ How to determine your values, interests, and aptitudes.

· ·

What type of job do you want? Before you answer that and begin your job search, you need to learn more about yourself. People differ in what they want from a job. Many people desire a high income. Some hope for fame. Others want adventure. Still others want to serve people and make the world a better place. Before you begin to explore job opportunities, you should determine (1) your values; (2) your interests; and (3) your aptitude. Most people are happiest on jobs that fit their values, interests, and aptitudes.

VALUES are deeply held beliefs that influence the way people think, act, and feel. They reflect what people consider to be important and greatly affect the goals people set for themselves. Each person has many values, which vary in strengths. For example, money is the strongest value for some people-that is, wealth is more important to them than anything else. As a result, they focus their thoughts, behavior, and emotions on the goal of earning a high income. Other values include devotion to religion, taking risks, spending time with family and helping others. People should understand their values prior to applying for a certain job.

You can develop an understanding of your values by asking yourself what is important to you and by examining your beliefs. For example, is it important for you to work as a member of a team? Or would you rather be in charge or work alone? If working alone or being in charge is important to you, independence is probably one of your primary values.

INTERESTS are related to values and typically are defined as likes or preferences. The subjects that you like in school and the leisure activities you prefer are indications of your interests. For example, someone who prefers working with others rather than alone would probably be interested in team sports or various other group activities. Many people have interests in artistic, mechanical, outdoor, or scientific activities. Others enjoy helping people and solving problems. Many people based their job choices on their interest. For numerous workers, job performance and job satisfaction depend on how much their work relates to their interests. It is therefore helpful to identify your strongest and most lasting interests before you select a job to apply for. To find out what your interests are, examine the kinds of activities you have enjoyed. Such activities might include club work, hobbies, and sports. The activities you enjoy most may represent your strongest interests.

APTITUDES are a person's natural talents. Aptitudes indicate how easily a person can acquire certain skills or be trained for a specific job. An aptitude is sometimes known as an ability. However, the term ability can also refer to a skill-such as reading or speaking a foreign language-that a person has learned. Before you apply for a certain job, you should determine if that job requires any special aptitudes. You should remember two important factors about aptitude. First, people may not realize they have certain aptitudes unless they are given the opportunity to develop them. Second, if you have relatively low aptitude in a given area, you can still develop the skills and abilities need to perform successfully in that area.

OTHER PERSONAL CHARACTERISTICS, such as friendliness, dependability, and honesty, can contribute to success on a job. They may even be essential elements of a job in sales, banking, management, or other fields. These kinds of characteristics are difficult to measure. However, taking a serious look back at your past behaviors can help you determine if you have such qualities.

After determining your values, interests, and aptitudes, list the type of jobs you feel you are best qualified for and want. List them in the order of your preference.

Once you have completed that list, you are ready for the next step - selecting your sources of job information.

Chapter 2

THE JOB SEARCH

· ·

In This Chapter You Will Learn

- ➢ Different Sources for finding available jobs.
- ➢ The power of networking.

· ·

Your first source of job information will probably be from friends,

neighbors, and relatives. Through their work, or social and business

contacts, they may know of opportunities not listed by regular sources.

But, of course, their knowledge is likely to be limited to their own and

perhaps a few other places of employment. At the same time you can

consult with personal sources, as well as the usual channels for job

information. Amongst the many sources, you will have to select those

most appropriate for you. That will depend on the type of job you

want, where you live and want to work, and the demand in your field.

IDENTIFYING POTENTIAL EMPLOYERS

Research is a critical part of the job search process. It can help you identify companies that may be hiring in your field. Focus your job search on employers whose values and expectations meet yours.

Get started! If you're just beginning your job search, visit the Employer Locator to identify and get contact information for potential employers in your local area.

Get focus! If you've already narrowed your job search list to a few prospective employees, or even scheduled interviews already, make sure to thoroughly explore those companies' web sites. These web sites will often include information such as a vision, mission statement, product descriptions, hiring policies, and job openings. Locate their web sites by entering the full name of the business into a search engine such as Google or Yahoo.

When you're looking at company web sites or conducting research at a library, try to answer some of the following basic questions (the answers will both increase your knowledge about a company and prepare you for classic interview questions such as "What can you tell us about this company?").

Question to think about when researching employers:

- ❖ What products/services does the employer provide?
- ❖ How many employees does the employer have?
- ❖ How long have they been in business?
- ❖ Where is the employer located?
- ❖ Does it have more than one location?
- ❖ What is the employer's mission statement or philosophy?
- ❖ What is the company's financial situation?
- ❖ Has the employer undergone any downsizing?
- ❖ Is the employer involved in any community services? If so, what?

THE BEST JOB SEARCH METHOD

If you don't already know the power of networking, you'll miss out on the vast majority of the job leads. Networking is often considered the most effective way to find a job and obtain an interview. Most companies would rather bring in a person that someone on their staff recommends for an interview before they go through the time and expense of paying for a classified ad, making multiple phone calls, and interviewing multiple people. You may be surprised to find that you know people who can give you information on unlisted job openings. They either work where you would like to work or know someone who works where you would like to work. It may be the person who sits next to you on your commute or the person in line behind you at the coffee shop. You never know when you may meet a potential contact, so always try to make a good first impression.

You can increase your odds of meeting contacts by talking regularly with your friends, neighbors, and former coworkers and by joining social groups, volunteer groups, and professional associations. Trade and professional organizations, as well as career fairs, are excellent ways to meet people working in the career you're pursuing. When you talk to contacts, demonstrate that you are informed about the field and are interested in what they have to say.

You should find an organized way to keep track of the people you've spoken with and any leads you've acquired. You can also make goals for how many people you want to contact in a day or in a week. Keep in mind that anyone who offers his or her assistance has earned the right to ask for yours in the future. Thanks you notes are a nice gesture to those who have given their time and advice. Also, any current coworkers who know about your job search should be held to confidentiality.

Another method of networking is to send your resume with a letter of inquiry to any company for which you are interested in working. You can see samples of job search letters in Appendix C.

 The letter should be very professional; you can use the standard letter or cover letter format. Address your letter to the Human Resources Director if you can find his or her name, or the equivalent person who would be in charge of hiring in your field of expertise. State what your interest is in the company and why you would like to work there. Do your research so that you sound familiar with their business. You can ask for your resume to be kept on file for future job openings if there are none available at the present. There may be a position open that you can interview for, but if you receive a letter of decline, call to thank the hiring manager for their time and consideration. While on the phone, ask politely if they know one or two people you could contact. You might be surprised that you can find additional contacts this way. If you make a good impression on the phone, the hiring manager may keep you in mind for future jobs. If they unwilling to give you an interview or contacts, they may consent to an informational interview for you to ask questions about the career and what hiring managers are looking for in candidates.

It is also a good idea to stay in touch with your contacts. Send a thank you note or email after you meet with someone. From time to time, continue to stay in touch with your network contacts to share information or to see if they have any new leads you can follow.

CONTACT EMPLOYERS DIRECTLY

One of the most effective methods for finding a job is making direct contact with employers. You can do this in many different ways:

1. USE THE TELEPHONE: You can learn about upcoming job openings by spending some time on the telephone. It's perfectly acceptable to "cold call" employers. In fact, this is the fastest way to get an interview. When you cold-call employers, always be polite and professional. Have a prepared outline of points to cover in front of you from which you (1) introduce yourself quickly (2) ask if they are hiring (3) ask if you can send your resume (4) get the person's name and thank them for their time and consideration.

2. POUNDING THE PAVEMENT/HITTING THE STREETS: Perhaps the oldest method of job-hunting and developing job leads, especially for entry-level positions and blue-collar job, is concentrating your job-search efforts in a specific geographic area literally going door-to-door and submitting job applications to employers. This method is especially useful if you are relocating because you make a trip prior to moving and spend that entire time submitting applications and meeting with prospective employers. Be sure to always dress professionally for those rare occasions where you may get interviewed(even briefly) on the spot.

3. COLD CONTACT/DIRECT MAIL: Cold contact has become somewhat of a lost art of job-hunting, but one that can still bring job-seekers great returns on the investment by uncovering the "hidden job market." This method of developing job leads involves the job-hunter compiling a list of potential employers. This list can come from numerous sources, including business and trade periodicals, company directories, even the phone book. Once you've collected the key research on each company (including the all-important name of the hiring manager for the position you are seeking), you mail out (either via postal mail or email) a specifically-tailored cover letter and resume to each employer. Note that you are not doing a 'mass mailing', but a targeted direct-mail campaign; mass mailings don't work.

MORE SOURCES OF JOB INFORMATION

JOB/CAREER FAIRS

Numerous types of career and job fairs occur regularly. Companies send employees to these fairs to meet and recruit top prospects. Your goal is to prepare beforehand and identify the key employers in attendance and then develop a strategy for breaking through the clutter of perhaps thousands of other job-seekers. And even if the employer is not in the market for someone with your mix of skills and experience, you can still get your foot in the door through this method.

One of the greatest strategies for career fair success is to obtain the list of organization attending the fair-- either from the fair's Website or brochure.

Once you have this list, the key is identifying the prospective employers that most interest you. Note: Don't immediately discount employers based on industry or perception (or misconceptions).

Finally, once you have made a list of the key (5-10) employers you want to meet at the fair, your task is to learn key facts about each of them so that you can showcase your knowledge to the recruiter(s). Examples of information you obtain (from the organization's Website, new organizations, and Internet searches):

- ❖ Organizational structure
- ❖ Key products/services
- ❖ Organizational culture and values

❖ Hiring practices

CLASSIFIED ADS

Newspaper classified ads were, at one time, the main source of job leads for job-seekers. However, as more companies now post job opening on their corporate sites and/or with online job sites, the importance of want ads has declined. Still, perusing want ads can be helpful for some types of job-seekers, particularly those seeking entry-level positions. It's worth noting, though, that career experts have never placed great value on job-seekers replying to want ads because many times these positions have been filled by the time the ads are published. Still, there is some value of scanning want ads, either in print or online.

PROFESSIONAL/TRADE ORGANIZATIONS

Every career field has at least one professional organization. Whether it's at the annual conference or an on-going process, most trade organizations offer some sort of job posting/resume exchange program. Find the process for getting the latest job postings and respond as soon you get them.

COLLEGE CAREER/ALUMNI OFFICES

One of the greatest benefits of a college degree--besides the degree itself--is joining an extremely large network of people that share one important element: your college or university. And regardless of the size of your alma mater, chances are pretty good that there are other alumni in your field who would be willing to help you advance your career. Contact the professionals from your alma mater's career services and/or alumni office and begin reaping one of the extended rewards of your college education. And if you're a current student, get over to those offices today and take advantage of all the services they offer.

CORPORATE CAREER CENTERS

One of the fastest growing sources of job leads has been the development of online corporate career(human resource) centers. Many companies, large and small, including just about all of the

Fortune 500 companies continue to build these corporate career centers--which often include job openings, guidelines for submitting job-search materials, and a wealth of information about the company(such as corporate culture, career paths, benefits, and more).

RECRUITERS/HEADHUNTERS

Another potentially good source for job leads is using the services of recruiters/headhunters. Only use those professional who are employed by companies to screen and select the most qualified candidates for positions the company has open. Avoid any employment agency where the applicant must pay the fee. Headhunters and recruiters are great sources of job leads as long as job-seekers remember like real estate agents, that these professionals work for the employer, not for you. And if you don't have the qualities their clients are looking for, they will not be interested in helping you get a foot in the door. There are numerous types of headhunters that often specialize by geographic region or by industry/profession.

TEMPORARY AGENCIES

You might also have temporary employment agencies in your area. Temporary work is ideal for those who would like to test out various potential employers to determine what kind of work environment might suit them best. While many temporary jobs may be clerical, they do give you an opportunity to show off your talents to employers and build references. Working as a temp may also put you in the right place at the right time when a great employment opportunity opens up at the company you are working for. You can gain valuable experience and make great contacts while working as a temp. Many temporary jobs lead to permanent employment.

INTERNSHIPS

Many people find jobs with business and organizations with whom they have interned or volunteered. Look for internships and volunteer opportunities on job boards, career centers, and company and association Websites, but also check community service organization and volunteer opportunity databases. Some internships and long-term volunteer positions come with stipends and all provide experience and the chance to meet employers and other good networking contacts.

BE PROACTIVE

Take the initiative to look for job openings that are not yet advertised. Sometimes employers hire people who contact them about employment opportunities. Some of these people may have heard about the job through networking; others simply send in their resume or contact the employer and inquire about job openings. As you attempt the various methods of searching for employment, remember that there are always positions out there for the people who are willing to find them.

RESUME

John B. Smith
111 Sylvan Ave., Englewood Cliffs, NJ 07632-1514
1-800-625-3999
johnsmith@mac.com

Profile Summary

- Experienced professional with a successful record of background business development and administration
- Excel at multi-task work, where it all levels to manage background business manual
- Proven specialty; have excelled in capturing and accomplishing organizational goals and expanding clientism
- Proven excellent interpersonal, analytical, and management skills; enjoy working in a team-driven setting
- An objective manager with the skill to recognize and implement a program with the ability to see in either program

Banking Employment   WOODGROVE B...

Chapter 3

PREPARING YOUR RESUME

. . . .

In This Chapter You Will Learn

- ❖ State the purpose of a resume and cover letter.
- ❖ List the contents of a resume.
- ❖ Identify the different types of resume formats.
- ❖ Explain your skills, interests, and abilities on your resume.
- ❖ Write an effective resume and cover letter.

. . . .

Most employers only spend about 6 seconds reviewing a resume.

Because of this, it's very important to write a resume and cover letter

that will impress a potential employer and capture his or her attention.

Employers often choose interview candidates based on these

documents. This chapter will provide tips on gathering the require

information for writing effective resumes.

RESUME

A resume is use to provide a summary of your skills, abilities and accomplishments. It is a quick advertisement of who you are. It is a "snapshot" of you with the intent of capturing and emphasizing interests and secures you an interview. Since your resume is a primary tool in your job search, it needs to be carefully written and critiqued. The purpose of a resume is to get an interview. There is no other way to say it. Resumes are one to two-page summaries of your qualifications and their sole purpose is to impress prospective employers. Your resume must be better than anything your competition has to offer if you are going to get an interview. If it is well-written, it will generate phone calls asking you to come in for interviews. If you are not getting phone calls and you are sending out resumes, then you need to take a closer look at what you are sending out. Any resume can list employment dates and job position titles, but only the best ones speak the language employers want to hear. You have to show them that you are cut above the rest of the crowd by providing concrete example of your successes. Do the thinking for the employer and give them what they are looking for.

CONTENT OF A RESUME

The resume content plays a major role in the selection of your resume for further rounds. Sometimes you might be the most qualified candidate for a particular position, but your resume fails to portray the same, and you might lose a good opportunity. Thus, the information portrayed in your resume is very crucial.

RESUMES SHOULD CONTAIN THE FOLLOWING INFORMATION:

❖ Your resume begins with your name and contact information (address, telephone number and your email address)

❖ Your past employers, listed in chronological order and beginning with the most recent, including addresses and length of time in each position

❖ Your education, usually in chronological order, beginning with the most recent

A RESUME MAY ALSO INCLUDE:

- ❖ An objective stating the type of job you're looking for

- ❖ Skills and Achievements

- ❖ Professional Information, such as honors, licenses and/or certifications, professional affiliations, and relevant hobbies

- ❖ Military service, for those who have served in the Armed Forces

- ❖ References

A RESUME SHOULD NOT INCLUDE:

- ❖ Sexuality or Gender

- ❖ Irrelevant job experiences

- ❖ Marital status

- ❖ Past salaries

YOUR RESUME SHOULD ANSWER THE FOLLOWING QUESTIONS FOR AN EMPLOYER

- ❖ What kind of training do you have?

- ❖ What skills do you have?

- ❖ What can you do?

❖ How long have you done it?

Your resume might be the only opportunity you get to sell yourself. Because your resume is so important, spend some time writing it. Following the steps below will help you write an effective resume.

STEP 1: FIND A JOB FOR YOUR RESUME

It's best to find a job you want to apply for(or at least figure out what type of job you want) before you write your resume. Why? Because your resume is a marketing piece for your job search, and the more you know about the job you want, the better you can target your resume. The first step in ensuring you add skills to your resume that align with those required by a specific position is to read the job posting carefully. Doing so not only shows you exactly what's required of the job but it also helps you to examine your own skills that match. It's also important to showcase your ability to learn new skills by highlighting previous training, along with a willingness to take on new projects. One way to do this is by listing any training course you've taken, certifications you've received, programs you're proficient in, and any other details that prove your ability to hit the ground running.

Don't let the lack of skills stop you, take the steps necessary to make your skills a perfect match for the job you deserve.

STEP 2: CHOOSE A RESUME FORMAT

If you don't choose the right format for your resume, you can easily doom your resume to the trash can. If you are changing careers, going back to work after years from the workplace or just starting out with very little experience, a chronological resume could be your worst enemy. Yet, if you have a solid history worth focusing on, then that same chronological resume could be the best way to present yourself.

RESUME FORMATS

There are three basic resume formats, functional, chronological and combination.

Functional: The functional resume draws attention to your skills instead of your past employment or work history by grouping relevant skills and accomplishments into special categories and placing them before the work history section of your resume.

Chronological: The chronological resume places more emphasis on your past employment by listing your work history near the beginning of your resume.

Combination: The combination resume combines the best features of the functional and chronological styles be emphasizing your abilities while including a full job history. This format is quickly becoming the format of choice for upwardly mobile professionals due to its flexibility and ability to highlight strengths and skills while allowing the use of searchable keywords near the beginning of the resume.

When choosing a resume format you have to ask, do I have direct, in-depth experience in the career I'm applying for?

If the answer is yes, then the traditional chronological resume format will serve you well. If your answer is no, the chronological format will emphasize the fact that you don't have the direct in-depth experience the employer is looking for. Your resume will hit the trash can.

If you do not have the direct in-depth experience, choose a functional resume format or a combination format instead. The functional resume format allows you to highlight the transferable skills you have that make you a good candidate for the job. In the resume format, your skills can be grouped into categories that parallel the skills description for the job posting. Functional resumes typically contain elements not used by chronological resumes: performance profiles, career objectives, qualifications summaries and relevant skill summaries. In addition, other sections may be added to coincide with your knowledge and circumstances.

The functional resume does have its drawbacks. Some employers see this format as an instant indicator that you are hiding something. In a way they are right. You are trying to de-emphasize your lack of experience in the specific job skills for the position. This is why you may want to consider the combination resume format.

If you do have direct, in-depth experience, a chronological resume format will emphasize your work history as directly relevant to the job you're seeking. If your experience demonstrates that you have grown within a single profession and without many job changes or periods of unemployment, then a chronological resume is a good choice. It combines your achievements and job-specific duties and applies them to each position with each employer in the work history section of your resume.

The combination resume format is used for a variety of situations:

- ❖ Those returning to the workforce after an extended absence
- ❖ Those who recently graduated from college
- ❖ Those possessing a wealth of knowledge with little true professional experience
- ❖ Those who have made many job changes and those who are embarking on a new career altogether

A combination resume combined the best of both the functional and the chronological formats. It allows you an opportunity to spotlight your credentials and your skills with self-awareness. The combination resume usually includes a professional profile or career summary to accentuate skills, trait and accomplishments. It may also include a job objective, a targeted job title or a positioning statement. This format utilizes a detailed skill summary and incorporates an area in which to highlight previous experiences and accomplishments in categories that

33

are relevant to both your job search and your personal history. The combination style also utilizes your work history, detailed in reverse chronological order, with the most recent experience listed first.

You can see samples of each type of resume format in Appendix C.

STEP 3: CONTACT INFORMATION

Your resume begins with your name and contact details. Use the form of your name as it appears on academic records and other documents an employer may require you to provide, so there will be no confusion that documents belong to the same person. Write your name at the center of the page in a font larger than the rest of the text and highlight it by using the "bold" option. The email address and postal address should be written below the name, followed by the contact number.

For Example:

DAVID KING
dave.king@yahoo.com
24 Country Club Drive
Jackson, TN 34750
Ph: 901-741-6250

NOTE: You should NOT have any email address such as sexygirl@yahoo or countryboy69@bellsouth or anything close to these. Email addresses like these will get your resume tossed very quickly.

STEP 4: CAREER OBJECTIVE

Your objective tells a prospective employer the type of work you are currently pursuing. The rest of your resume should be designed to mostly effectively support your objective. It should include the type of work you are seeking and what skills you wish to utilize.

Objectives aren't always included on a resume. If your resume is lengthy, you don't have to include an objective. However, if your experience and/or education is limited, you might want to include an objective.

The standard formula for developing an objective statement is this:

To obtain a position as a_____ in the _____ industry, utilizing my _____,_____, and _____ skills.

STEP 5: EDUCATION

The education section of your resume lists any education you received in chronological order, beginning with the most recent. Most of the time, your education section will follow the objective statement. This is because your education is usually related to your objective. Most education sections includes the following information:

- ❖ Dates of training or date of graduation
- ❖ Diploma/Degree obtained
- ❖ School name, city, state, and zip code
- ❖ Relevant courses taken

The following in an example of an Education section:

Associate Degree in Paralegal Studies (2000)

Southwest Community College, Baton Rouge, LA 70806

Completed course in legal research, family law, business law, criminal law and legal writing

STEP 6: WORK EXPERIENCE

This is by far the most important section of your resume. You should spend more time on this section. Make sure that you list your job in order, beginning with either your current job or most recent job if you are currently unemployed.

Most work experience section includes the following:

- ❖ Name of the company
- ❖ City and state of the company
- ❖ Job title
- ❖ Employment dates
- ❖ Description of duties and responsibilities

The following in an example of a Work experience section:

12/11-12/13 EXECUTIVE HOUSEKEEPER

Best Western Hotel, Woodville, MS 39669

Supervised 30 rooms, hired housekeeping personnel, and purchased all supplies and equipment

Tailor your resume for the specific job that you want. Tailoring your resume requires you to emphasize on your experiences to make you seem especially qualified for the job.

STEP 7: SUMMARY OF QUALIFICATION

This section is used to highlight the skills you posse that would make you an excellent candidate for the job. You should have at least three but no more than five brief items that you feel will set you apart from other applicants and demonstrate your strongest assets. Always read the job description first, than state skills and experience that is being sought by the employer.

The following are a few examples of qualification summary:

❖ Excellent communication and customer services skills

❖ Work well with supervisor and other co-workers

❖ Work quickly and proficiently under daily deadlines in a fast-pace environment.

STEP 8: KEEP YOUR RESUME SIMPLE

Your resume should appear professional as well as easy to read. Don't underline words, use boldface or italics instead- and use them sparingly. Use good-quality 8 1/2 x 11 paper, printed on one side, so that it will be easier to scan. White, cream or gray paper is best. Never use colored paper, it's unacceptable. Unless you have over ten years of work experience, resumes should only be one page long. More than one page will probably be discarded because employers do not want to spend the extra time on unnecessary information.

STEP 9: PROOFREAD AND REVISE

Proofread your resume carefully and have someone proofread it also. Make changes when needed.

STEP 10: CREATE AN ONLINE VERSION OF YOUR RESUME

People are looking for work more these days online. Because of this, it's a great idea to prepare an online version of your resume that you can send in an email.

The following are tips for creating an online resume:

- ❖ Don't use fancy font, boldface or underlining in online resumes. Different computers may interpret these techniques differently. An online resume should be formatted very simply.
- ❖ Dashes, quotation marks, and bullets usually don't work in an online resume. While you can produce these marks with a standard word processing program, e-mail programs sometimes translate them into other signs.

The following signs usually work on online resumes and are often used instead of bullets and other signs:

- ❖ Hyphen -
- ❖ Plus sign +
- ❖ Single and double asterisks * **

Whenever possible, paste your resume into e-mail message instead of attaching it. Some employers won't open or download attachments because they're afraid of computer viruses. And including your resume in an e-mail message eliminates an extra step for an employer who's probably fatigued from reviewing many resumes.

Keep your online resume very short. Employers probably won't bother scrolling down to read a lengthy resume.

COVER LETTERS

You just learned that the goal of a resume is to convince an employer to call you for an interview. The goal of a cover letter sometimes called a job application letter is to convince an employer to read your resume. A cover letter is a letter of introduction that states the reason you're writing to an employer. Like resumes, cover letters are marketing tools; they explain why you are the perfect person for the job. They should be brief, well written, and easy to read. Writing a good cover letter is as important as writing a good resume.

Following the steps in this section will help you write an effective cover letter.

STEP 1: ADD A LETTERHEAD AT THE TOP OF THE LETTER

Your letterhead should include your full name, address, telephone number, and email address. Some guidelines to follow when creating your letterhead:

❖ Your name should be in bold 14- or 16- point font.

❖ Your address and other contact information should be in normal 12-point font.

❖ The font of your letterhead does not need to be Arial or Times New Roman, like the rest of your letter, but it should be professional looking and easy to read. The most important thing to remember is to include up-to-date information so that you make it easy for the employer to contact you. You may want to include an extra line under the letterhead in order to create visual appeal and to separate the letterhead from the rest of the letter.

STEP 2: WRITE THE RECIPIENT'S NAME AND ADDRESS AND THE DATE BELOW THE LETTERHEAD

It doesn't matter whether you put the date first or last, or how many blank lines you include between them, as long as it looks professional. From here on out, use 12-point Arial or Times New Roman throughout the entire letter, set your margins to one inch, and use single spacing. Be sure your font is black, and if you're printing your letter out, use standard-sized paper (8 1/2" by 11").

STEP 3: ADDRESS THE RECIPIENT

Be sure to refer to the recipient by his or her proper title (Mrs., Mr., Dr., etc.). If you're not sure who the recipient is write, "To Whom It May Concern:" or "Dear Sir or Madam"; however, it is always best to address a cover letter to a real person to make it look like you're not sending form letters.

STEP 4: STATE YOUR PURPOSE IN THE FIRST PARAGRAPH

Tell the employer why you are writing to them in two or three sentences. States the position for which you are applying (or the one you would like to have should it become available). You don't necessarily need to include how you became aware of the position unless it was through mutual contact or recruiting program in case you should make the most of the connection. If you are writing a letter of interest (also known as a prospecting or inquiry letter) in which you are asking about positions that might be available, specify why you are interested in working for the employer.

STEP 5: OUTLINE YOUR QUALIFICATIONS IN THE MIDDLE PARAGRAPH(S)

Make sure to match them to the requirements of the position. If you are writing to inquire about open positions, tell the employer how you can contribute to their bottom line, not what you want to get out of the deal. To do this, use what you have researched about the employer's background and history. Make your qualifications jump out at the reader by researching the company to which you are applying for a job and tailoring your letter accordingly. This will also be useful if you get an interview. Some questions to keep in mind as you write are:

1. What is the employer's mission?

2. What do they promote as the one thing that sets them apart from their competitors?

STEP 6: INCLUDE A POSITIVE STATEMENT OR QUESTION IN THE FINAL PARAGRAPH THAT WILL MOTIVATE THE EMPLOYER TO CONTACT YOU

Make this closing paragraph between two to four sentences. Direct the employer to your enclosed resume and make sure you specify that you're available for an interview. Finish off by thanking the recruiter for their time and consideration, and welcome them to get in touch with you to continue the conversation.

STEP 7: WRITE AN APPROPRIATE CLOSING

It's a good idea to thank the reader for his or her time. After that, write "Sincerely," "Respectfully," or "Regards," leave several spaces, and print your name.

STEP 8: ADD YOUR SIGNATURE

If you will be submitting your cover digitally, it's a good idea to scan and add your signature, write it in with a digital writing pad, or make a digital signature stamp with appropriate software.

STEP 9: MAKE SURE TO COMPLETE A SPELL CHECK TO CORRECT ANY MISSPELLED WORDS

STEP 10: READ YOUR LETTER ALOUD TO SEE HOW IT READS.

You can see a sample of a cover letter in Appendix C.

YOUR RESUME IS YOUR SALES PITCH

Remember that your resume, combined with your cover letter, is your only opportunity to sell yourself. If you can accomplish this task in one page, do your best to do so. At the same time, it's often not possible to present yourself effectively in one page, especially if you have a solid work history to present.

Employers do want to see some form of work history, even if it includes volunteer and self-employment positions. Yet, someone starting out new or changing career may have never worked in a job related to the position he or she is applying for. This is why it is so important to study the job description.

If the employer provides very little detail, a call or an email asking for more information about the job, could be your opportunity to stand out. Mention that you want to be sure you have the right qualifications for the position. You never know whether this indication that you are serious about being valuable to your future employer may just land you the job.

Chapter 4

INTERVIEWING

· ·

In This Chapter You Will Learn

> ➤ The types of interviews.
> ➤ How to dress for an interview.
> ➤ Common questions asked in an interview.
> ➤ Proper and Improper interview behaviors.
> ➤ Questions you should ask during an interview.

· ·

A job interview is your showcase for marketing your skills. During the interview, an employer judges your qualifications, appearance, and general fitness for the job opening. It is your opportunity to convince the employer that you can make a real contribution. Equally important, it gives you a chance to appraise the job, the employer, and the company. It enables you to decide if the job meets your career needs and interests and whether the company is the right fit for you.

TYPES OF INTERVIEWS

If possible, ask your prospective employer what type of interview you will have. This will help you prepare and feel more confident. Types of interviews include:

- ❖ ONE-ON-ONE: just you and one interviewer, the most common type of interview

- ❖ PANEL: more than one person interviews you at the same time

- ❖ GROUP: you are not the only applicant in the room; usually a group of candidates is interviewed by a panel

- ❖ MEAL: you are interviewed while eating, usually over lunch

- ❖ WORKING: you are put to work and observed

- ❖ TELEPHONE: often used as a screening tool before inviting you to an on-site interview

- ❖ ON-SITE or SECOND ROUND: after you have made it through a screening interview, many organizations will invite you to their site for an extended interview that may include a series of different types of interviews, a site tour, and a meal.

Getting a second round interview means the organization is seriously considering you for a position.

PREPARING FOR A PHONE INTERVIEW

- ❖ Schedule it for a time when you can give it 100 percent of your attention and take the call in a quiet place

- ❖ Jot down points you want to make, a list of your skills and accomplishments with examples, and question to ask

- ❖ Keep a copy of your resume and the job description near the phone

- ❖ Have your calendar in front of you if you need to set up another interview

- ❖ Ask for clarification if necessary and think out your responses clearly before you answer

- ❖ Show enthusiasm for the position-be sure to smile-it can come through your voice

- ❖ Avoid saying, "ah, er, um." These non-words are more noticeable on the phone

PREPARING FOR A SECOND ROUND INTERVIEW

❖ Confirm the date, time, location, and who you should ask for on arrival.

❖ Make any necessary travel arrangements.

❖ Keep any receipts. Most medium are large companies will pay for your expenses.

❖ Research the company ahead of time. The employer will expect you to be very familiar with them.

❖ Study the job description and know exactly what you are interviewing for.

❖ Bring an extra copy of your resume.

❖ Bring at least five questions to ask. Develop lists of different question tailored to who you are meeting with.

❖ Be prepared to answer the same question several times. During the day you will most likely meet several people; your potential supervisor, coworker and a human resources representative. They may ask you the same questions. Be enthusiastic, honest, and consistent in your answers.

❖ Remember that you are always being evaluated. In group activities and during meals.

❖ Remember that an interview is a two-way street. Be observant.

❖ Remember to ask when you can expect to hear from the employer again.

❖ Know what to do if you receive an offer on the spot. In most cases, it's better to think about the offer before accepting or declining.

HOW TO DRESS FOR AN INTERVIEW

While a polished and professional outfit is no substitute for a killer resume, the right look can set you apart from other jobseekers and boost your confidence. The first impression you make on a potential employer is the most important one. The first judgment an interviewer makes is going to be based on how you look and what you are wearing. That's why, in many cases, it is still important to dress professionally for the job interview, regardless of the work environment.

MEN'S INTERVIEW ATTIRE

❖ **DARK SUIT**- Dark blue, black or grey is the best colors to wear to an interview.

❖ **LONG SLEEVE SHIRT**- A white long sleeve shirt shows a very professional look. You can get by with other light colors shirt only if they coordinated well with you suit.

❖ **PLAIN TIE**- Keep your tie plain and simple.

❖ **DARK SOCKS**- Black is the best color for your socks.

❖ **DARK POLISHED CONSERVATIVE SHOES**- Make sure the shoes that you wear are clean and traditional. Nothing can leave a worse impression than a person wearing dirty shoes to an interview.

❖ **LITTLE OR NO JEWELRY**- If you usually wear an earring take it out before the interview. Wearing a watch and wedding band is acceptable.

❖ **HAIR**- Your hair should be neat and freshly washed and trimmed. Facial hair should be shaved clean with the exception of a neat mustache.

- ❖ **NAILS-** Your nails should be trimmed and clean.

- ❖ **COLOGNE-** While smelling good is always a plus; make sure that you do not drench yourself in cologne as it can have a detrimental effect.

WOMEN'S INTERVIEW ATTIRE

- ❖ **Dark Suit or Dress-** The most common attire for a woman is a navy, black, or grey suit. Dress slacks, dresses, and skirts are acceptable too.

- ❖ **BLOUSE-** A woman should wear a plain white or other pale color blouse to an interview.

- ❖ **PANTYHOSE-** Women should wear dark or nude colored nylon pantyhose. It's always good to carry an extra pair in case the rip or tear.

- ❖ **SHOES-** Women should wear low heels or flats to an interview. For women, wearing unprofessional and uneasy shoes gives the wrong signal. When you show up for a job interview, your entire persona should exude professionalism so that the employers get the right message.

- ❖ **JEWELRY**- A classy matching necklace, bracelet, ring, and 1 pair of earring should be your limit.

- ❖ **PERFUME**- Avoid excessive perfume because it could be overpowering and distracting. Make sure you choose to use a subtle fragrance so that it does not irritate the interviewer.

- ❖ **MAKEUP**- Use it to lightly highlight certain features and cover up blemishes. Avoid creating a mask that is alluring and so different that interviewer won't recognize you when you see him or her again.

- ❖ **HAIR**- Your hair should be freshly washed and neatly styled. It is ideal to wear your hair up rather than leaving it down.

- ❖ **PURSE**- Leave your purse in the car or at home. It's always good to carry either a portfolio or briefcase

WHAT TO BRING TO AN INTERVIEW

It's important to go on a job interview prepared with everything you need, organized and ready to go. Here is a list of the things you need:

- ❖ **DIRECTIONS**- If you're not sure where you're going bring direction and any instruction the hiring manager may have given you. If you have an email confirmation of the appointment bring that too.

❖ **IDENTIFICATION-** If the building has security you may be asked to show identification. You may also need it to complete a job application, so bring your Driver's License or another form of identification with you to the interview.

❖ **NOTEPAD AND PENS -** It's easier to have your own pen than to borrow one if you have to fill out paperwork. Also bring a notepad so you can jot down names and company information.

❖ **NAME OF CONTACTS -** Write down the name of the person you're interviewing with on your notepad. It can be easy to forget a name and you don't want to be embarrassed.

❖ **LIST OF QUESTIONS TO ASK -** Have a list of questions to ask the interviewer. If need be, you can skim it quickly when you're asked if you have questions.

❖ **EXTRA COPIES OF YOUR RESUME -** Bring several copies of your resume to give out upon request. Your resume will also give you the details like dates of employment you need if you have to fill out a paper job application.

- ❖ **REFERENCE LIST-** Bring a printed list of references to give to the hiring manger. Include at least three professional references and their contact information, who can attest to your ability to perform the job you are applying for, on your list.

- ❖ **A PORTFOLIO-** A portfolio is a great way to package all the items you're bringing with you to the interview in a neat and orderly fashion. That way, you're organized and everything you need will be readily accessible.

WHAT NOT TO BRING TO A JOB INTERVIEW

What you shouldn't bring to the job interview is important too. Here is a list of what not to bring:

- ❖ Gum or candy
- ❖ Coffee, soda, or water
- ❖ Cell phone
- ❖ A hat or cap
- ❖ Too many rings

❖ Family or friends

PROPER AND IMPROPER INTERVIEW BEHAVIOR

There are many things that you can do to take some of the pressure off during an interview. The way you behave is one of the most important. It's not all the words that come out of your mouth, but often has a lot to do with the mannerism you use. Interviews are not just about if you are skilled enough for the job, they are often about if you would fit nicely with your co-workers. Your personality is a big part of your interview and can make all of the difference in the world. Below is a list of dos and don'ts to follow during an interview:

❖ **DO** arrive early, but not more than ten or fifteen minutes. There is no excuse for being late. Leave home extra early if you have to. Blaming it on the traffic or anything else doesn't matter (even if it's true).

❖ **DO** be polite to everyone when you get to the interviewer's office. While waiting to be interviewed, sit properly and behave as if everyone passing you by is your potential interviewer. They just might be! Smile at people as much as

61

possible. Do not act impatient or bored, it sends the wrong message. Some interviewers will keep you waiting just to see how you handle yourself.

❖ **DO** remain standing until your interviewer asks you to be seated. It is simply polite and shows proper etiquette.

❖ **DO** maintain good eye contact at all times. Keeping eye contact with your interviewer is very important, especially when one of you is speaking to the other. If you are looking around the room or at item on the interviewer's desk you will appear uninterested.

❖ **DO** sit up straight and speak with confidence. Be sure of your abilities without appearing cocky or narcissistic. You want to let the interviewer know that you are equipped to perform well at your job without alienating other co-workers. Point out your accomplishment in your field while remaining somewhat humble.

❖ **DO** take the time to answer an interviewer's question. If you need some time to think before you answer take it. You don't want to look stuck and allow long periods of silence, but thinking about a question before you commit to an answer shows the interviewer that you're careful and that you care about your answers. Don't answer questions with "yes" or "no". Explain your reasons for answering a question in a certain way.

❖ **DO** ask the interviewer questions you've prepared ahead of time. Asking thoughtful questions is an excellent way to show your interest in the position and demonstrate that you have done research on the company.

❖ **DON'T** eat or drink anything while waiting to be interviewed.

❖ **DON'T** chat on your cell phone while waiting for your interviewer. It makes you look distracted.

❖ **DON'T** ever say negative things about your previous boss. It shows a lack of respect for your superior. They may have been the worst boss in the world but expressing that in a job interview is a huge mistake.

❖ **DON'T** shrug your shoulders when asked a question that you are unsure of. Take a second to think of your response. Shrugging your shoulders give the impression that you don't know the answer.

❖ **DON'T** lie about past jobs. An interviewer can easily verify previous job information. Lying will show the interviewer that you're not trustworthy and you probably want get the job.

❖ **DON'T** get sucked in to talking about money. An Interviewee who is overly concerned about salary and benefits probably won't get hired especially if the interviewer thinks he or she is expecting too much.

❖ **DON'T** ever turn down a job at the interview, even if you know you don't want to work there. Keep your options open. If you do want the job, make sure the interviewer knows this before you leave. Tell him or her how much you enjoyed the interview and how impressed you are with the company.

❖ **DON'T** leave the interview without shaking the interviewer's hand a second time. Wait until your interviewer stands up or requests that you do. Give your closing greeting. Thank the interviewer for taking the time to see you. Offer another firm handshake and ask when you might expect to hear from them about their decision.

COMMON INTERVIEW QUESTIONS

Many interviewers will ask standard questions during an interview. Knowing some of the questions before an interview will give you time to prepare good answers and force you to think about how you're going to present yourself in the interview. Below is a list of standard interview questions and tips for good responses:

❖ **Can you tell me a little about yourself?**

This question seems simple, so many people fail to prepare for it, but it's crucial. Here's the deal: Don't give your complete employment (or personal) history. Instead give a pitch that's concise and compelling and that shows exactly why you're the right fit for the job. Start off with the 2-3 specific accomplishments or experience that you want the interviewer to know about, wrap up talking about how that prior experience has positioned you for this specific role.

❖ **Why are you looking for a new job?**

Interviewers often present this question, and it can be a trap. Don't fall into it by talking about the horrors of your previous job or employer.

65

Steer you answer away from negativity and instead talk about new opportunities, more challenges, more room for advancement, and a chance to use your skills to their full capability. Many times during your answer an interviewer might attempt to throw you off by asking what was wrong with your last job, or why you couldn't fully implement your skills while working there. Focus on skills you have that aren't required for your current position but that may be required in the position you're interviewing for. While talking about your current job, describe your duties with enthusiasm.

❖ **What are your greatest strengths and weaknesses?**

View this as an opportunity to point out your strengths that relate to being successful in the position for which you are interviewing. Back up your statements with examples of experiences in which you have demonstrated your strengths. Strategies for addressing a weakness (only mention one) include choosing one you have overcome, or selecting an area/skill that you have not had much time to develop or an area that is not important to the demands of the work. Also, be genuine with your answers and avoid cliché answers such as "I work too hard" or "I'm a perfectionist." Employers are impressed by people who can be honest, recognize area for improvement, and overcome personal challenges.

❖ What do you do in you spare time?

This question gives you a little bit more freedom to talk about yourself on a personal level. Interviewers asking this question want to get an idea how well rounded you are. Talk about your hobbies, but don't mention anything that could remotely be considered negative. The interviewer just wants to know what you're like when you're away from the workplace. Mention if you read, go for long drives, spend time with your family, or eat at exotic restaurants. Show the interviewer that you're an interesting person, but avoid discussing your eccentricities.

❖ Why was there a gap in your employment?

If you were unemployed for a period of time, be direct and to the point about what you've been up to (and hopefully, that's a list of impressive volunteering and other mind-enriching activities, like blogging or taking classes). Then, steer the conversation toward how you will do the job and contribute to the organization. "I decided to take a break at the time, but today I'm ready to contribute to this organization in the following ways."

❖ **What are your salary requirements?**

Say that you expect nothing more than fair compensation for your job and avoid naming actual figures. Related to this question, an interviewer may also ask how much you're currently being paid or how much you were paid at your last job. Be honest!

❖ **How would your boss and co-workers describe you?**

First of all, be honest (remember, if you get this job, the hiring manager will be calling your former bosses and co-workers).Then, try to pull out strengths and traits you haven't discussed in other aspects of the interview, such as your strong work ethic or willingness to pitch in on other projects when needed.

❖ **Do you have any questions for us?**

You probably already know that an interviewer isn't just a chance for a hiring manager to grill you it's your opportunity to sniff out whether a job is the right fit for you. What do you want to know about the position? The company? The department? The team?

QUESTIONS YOU SHOULD ASK IN AN INTERVIEW

Bring a least five questions to ask employers to all of your interviews. Asking thoughtful questions is a professional way to show your interest in the position and demonstrate that you have done research on the company. Avoid questions that you can find the answers to on the company's website and focus on questions that show you have gone above and beyond to learn about the employer through news articles, company reports, talking to company representative, etc. It is usually OK to ask question during the interview, and typically the interviewer will ask you if you have any questions at the end of the interview. Although questions will vary with each interview, the following are some possible question to ask:

- ❖ **ALWAYS ASK**: May I have your business card(s)? This will give you proper contact information for thank you letter and follow-up information.

- ❖ **ALWAYS ASK**: What are the next steps in the hiring process? This will give you a timeline, peace of mind, and clues for any possible follow-up actions.

- ❖ When and how are employees evaluated?

- ❖ What are the best/worst aspects of working in this organization?

- ❖ What the biggest challenge facing this organization right now?

- ❖ How would you compare your organization with your major competitors?

- ❖ How would you describe this organization's management style?

- ❖ What is the career path for my position?

- ❖ What kind of training is given to new employees?

QUESTIONS TO AVOID IN AN INTERVIEW

- ❖ **Never ask** for information you could have easily found with a quick internet search.

- ❖ **Never ask** if you can change the job details, the schedule, or the salary.

- ❖ **Never ask** question about the interviewer's background.

- ❖ **Never ask** about pay, time off, benefits, etc.

- ❖ **Never ask** "What does your company do?"

- ❖ **Never ask** "If I'm Hired, when can I start applying for other positions in the company?"

- ❖ **Never ask** how quickly you can be promoted.

- ❖ **Never ask** "Do you do background checks?"

- ❖ **Never ask** about gossip you've heard.

- ❖ **Never ask** if the company monitors e-mail or internet usage.

AFTER THE INTERVIEW

Every interview is a learning experience, so after the interview, ask yourself the following questions to prepare for your next one:

- ❖ How did my interview go?

- ❖ Did I feel at ease with the interviewer after my initial nervousness?

- ❖ Did I highlight how my experience and skills could meet with their qualifications?

- ❖ Did I ask questions which helped me clarify the position and show my interest and knowledge?

- ❖ Did I take the opportunity to mention my strengths and show what I have to offer?

- ❖ Was I positive and enthusiastic?

- ❖ How did I make myself stand out?

- ❖ What points did I make that seemed to interest the interviewer?

- ❖ Did I talk too much? Too little? Was I aggressive; not aggressive enough?

❖ What did I learn that I can apply to my next interview? How can I improve the next time?

SENDING A THANK YOU

Regardless how you think the interview went, it is customary for people to send a thank you email or letter to the interviewer within 24-48 hours of the interview. Always address the interviewer by name and thank him or her for the opportunity to interview. Indicate what you particularly enjoyed from the day's events and how the interview experience strengthens your interest in the position and organization.

Here is a sample of a thank you email:

> Dear Mr. Scott:
>
> I would like to thank your for meeting with me on yesterday. The discussion we had was particularly informative. I found the tour of the school and the informal conversation with your Principal to be quite beneficial. After the interview my enthusiasm for working at your school has increased. Please feel free to contact me if you have any more questions.
>
> Thanks you for your time and consideration and I look forward to hearing from you.
>
> > Sincerely,
> > David Carter

Employment Application

Personal Details:

Date of Application:	
Name of Applicant:	
Address (street, city, State Zip):	

Personal Contact:

House Telephone Number:	
Cell Phone Number:	
Email address:	

How did you get to know the company?

Applied Position:	
Date willing to begin work:	
Expected salary range:	

Are you currently in employment?

Education background

Please list the institutions attended and your qualifications beginning with the most recent in the space provided.

Feel free to add in the space provided below your special skills if any and how they would contribute to the performance of the job applied for

Chapter 5

JOB APPLICATION

. . . .

In This Chapter You Will Learn

 ➢ How to complete an application
 ➢ What to leave off an application
 ➢ What a reference list should include.

. . . .

Most employers ask job applicants to fill out an application form. Such forms help employers find out about your qualifications. Job application forms should be filled out carefully. Make your answer as brief, neat, and complete as possible.

Most application forms request the same kinds of information, and much of the information duplicates that given in resumes. The applications ask for address, telephone number, social security number, and the title of the job for which you are applying for. Most applications also ask about your previous employment, including your employers' and supervisors' names, the dates of your employment, and your duties. The application further request that you list the schools you attended, the dates you attended them, and any degrees, diplomas, and certificates you received. Many applications will request information about military experience, health, and hobbies. They may also ask for the names and addresses of personal references.

HOW TO FILL OUT A JOB APPLICATION

Filling out a job application should be a fairly simple process if you put together the information ahead of time. The most important part of any job application is your work history. Many applicants make the common mistake of thinking that excluding pertinent contact information or job history specifics is no big deal; this couldn't be farther from the truth. In fact, incorrectly or incompletely filling out a job application can cost you the opportunity to get the job of your dreams. Here are some tips on how to correctly fill out a job application so you can avoid some of the more common pitfalls of this process.

Fill in your own contact information first. Be sure this information is up to date and correct, as this is how a potential employer will contact you for a job. Be complete when listing your address, and include all of your phone numbers as well as your email address. If you are listing multiple phone numbers, it is important to note what kind of numbers they are: cell, work, home, friend, family member. Read over this information carefully before submitting your application to be sure that the numbers listed are correct and haven't been accidentally transposed.

Employment desired. You should never put words like "any" or "asap" on your application because you will appear too desperate. No matter how desperate you are for a job, you do not want this desperation to come out on your application. Employers are looking to hire applicants who show interest in their company, not applicants who will do anything for a paycheck.

Fill in other specifics, such as educational background and special certifications. Don't just list that you have a bachelor's degree. List the name, address, phone number and Web site of the university from which you received the degree and the specialty you majored in. If you have more than one degree, you must list this information for all of them. Being thorough not only helps potential employers get references and background information easily, but it also makes you look just that much more efficient and organized.

Give a complete accounting of your employment history. Not only should you list dates, job titles and specific responsibilities, but you should also highlight awards, special commendations and anything else that made you stand out as a star employee during your tenure with the company. List your supervisors and their contact information, including phone number and email addresses. If you changed positions during your time at a particular company, start with your original position and list your changing job titles as you worked your way up the career ladder. Some applicants may not have room for you to list some of this information. If this is the case, in the interest of filling out the form as completely as possible, attach a copy of your resume to the application so potential employers will have a full accounting of your employment history.

Write neatly, answer questions in complete sentences and try to answer every question cr query on the application. If there are things on it that don't apply to you, then simply write in "Not Applicable" or "N/A." Be sure to write as neatly as possible and take your time filling out the application to minimize the amount of mistakes. If you make a mistake and aren't too far into the application, start over, if you have an extra copy. If not, carry white-out with you to properly erase your mistake. You might also consider using an erasable pen to fill out job applications. Answer questions concisely and with the most amount of information in the least amount of words.

WHAT SHOULD YOU LEAVE OFF AN APPLICATION

You don't need to tell all to an employer. Sometimes, what you choose to leave off your applications is as important as what you include. Along with not revealing why you left a job or if you were fired, here are some other things you should keep to yourself to avoid damaging your chances.

❖ Any hint that you're unsure about the job or your career choice

Your application should position you for the role. This means you can present your work history in any way or format you want, in order to highlight the most relevant or outstanding details for that job. Be clear (in your cover letter and at interview) why the job and company appeal to you, and how they fit your career goals. If you're a recent graduate with a diverse work history or an unrelated degree, you'll need to explain why you think this role is the perfect match for your skills and interests.

❖ Lack of confidence in your abilities

Most employers want someone who can work with minimum supervision. Don't reveal a lack of confidence about the crucial, technical elements of the role. Read the job description and person specification thoroughly so you can prepare solid examples of how you'll deploy vital skills or demonstrated key personal qualities. At the interview, be prepared for "strengths/weakness" type of questioning. Answer honestly; admit to (minor) shortcomings to demonstrate self-awareness; but then say how you're rectifying the situation.

❖ Academic failure

Some companies insist on a solid history of achievement. But many others go straight to your experience section, overlooking academic qualifications. Don't let any educational shortcomings discount you; you don't need to broadcast a failed module or year, or poorer marks than expected.

❖ Illness

Avoid mentioning previous physical or mental illness in your initial applications. You can discuss any special arrangements you might need to carry out your job at interview.

❖ Demands

If you're applying for a full-time role, don't apply asking for part-time hours. Likewise, if you're applying for one type of role, don't drop heavy hints that you'd rather be interviewing for another.

❖ Inability to get on with others

Personality and attitude are crucial elements in candidate selection, so admitting that you found it hard to create good working relationships will raise red flags. Avoid criticizing previous managers. Instead, emphasize how difficult decisions were made mutually and make sure no note of bitterness creeps in.

You can see a sample job application in Appendix E

REFERENCES

References are people who can verify your work ethic, character and reliability to your prospective employers. Some applications will not include a section for your references, so you should be prepared to provide a list. Former teachers, supervisors and managers are your best professional references. Always get your references permission before you list them.

Reference List contains the following information:

- ❖ Name
- ❖ Job Title
- ❖ Company
- ❖ Work Phone
- ❖ Email

A Reference List may also include:

- ❖ Number of years known

- ❖ Experience/Skills of yours that this reference is familiar with

- ❖ Relationship to You

You can see a sample of a Reference List in Appendix C

TWO REASONS NOT TO GIVE REFERENCES OUT PRIOR TO AN INTERVIEW

1. You want an opportunity to evaluate the position, learn the criteria, and determine whether this a position you are interested in. The last thing you want to do is allow your valuable references to be contacted by so many companies that your references lose interest and enthusiasm. Some of these potential employers may not even be contenders for your interest

2. After an interview, you'll have an opportunity to contact your references (prior to the potential employer's call) and fill them in on the key points and issues of importance to the particular position. When you prepare your references, they will be more relaxed and

ready to provide the type of information you want them to give for the

specific job in question.

5. After _____ ... proven free of _____

Reference: _____

a. 15 _____
b. the average operating _____
c. 70% of operating _____
d. 125.5 mg

IV. Answer Section:

A	B	C	D
1			

A	B	C	D
2			

_____ following answer key may _____

Chapter 6

TESTING FOR A JOB

. . . .

In This Chapter You Will Learn

➢ How to prepare for a job test.

➢ Why employers drug test.

➢ The legal limits on drug testing.

. . . .

Many firms require a standardized test, or a series of such tests, as part of the application procedure. The tests most commonly used are those that show intelligence or general aptitude. In addition, some companies use tests that give them information on specific aptitudes, personality traits, and interest patterns.

Employers use literacy tests, also called cognitive tests, as part of the process to screen and select applicants for employment and promotion. While aptitude tests gauge your ability to learn and perform the tasks of the job, the literacy test measures your general reading and math levels. The employer wants to know if you can read and comprehend English, and perform basic math as part of your normal job duties. Your Literacy test may be a straightforward reading and math test or it could include elements to test other abilities and knowledge.

Many employers require job applicants to take a drug test also; particular those applicants who have reached the final stages on the selection process.

PREPARING TO TAKE A TEST FOR A JOB

If you are a recent graduate, you are probably used to taking tests. But if you have been away from school for some years, you may be apprehensive about the testing process. You may fear that your test scores will not reflect your ability to do a job. Don't let tests scare you off. Few of the commonly used tests require advance preparation; you need not feel concerned over not having "crammed" the night before. And bear in mind that your scores are only one among the many factors the employer will consider in judging your job qualifications.

Many tests have time limits. When they do, you will be told how much time you will have. Listen carefully to the instructions you receive. If you do not clearly understand what you are expected to do, be sure to ask questions. The time for questions, however, is before the test begins. If the test is timed, seconds lost in asking questions after it starts could seriously affect your score. After you start the test, work steadily and carefully. Do not let anything interrupt your work. In taking most tests, you should not spend too much time on any one question; instead, come back to difficult or time-consuming ones after you have completed the others. Remember, however, that some tests do not penalize for wrong answers, and a blank answer is counted as wrong.

Once the test is over, do not reproach yourself for not doing better. If the test is well constructed, you probably would make a similar score if you took it again.

Remember, too, that employers do not regard your score as an infallible measure of your abilities-- but as only one indication of them.

You can see a sample Job Aptitude Test in Appendix F.

WHY EMPLOYERS DRUG TEST

Most private employers are not required to test for alcohol or drug use. The big exception to this rule is for transportation and other safety-sensitive industries that are regulated by certain federal agencies such as the Federal Highway Administration, the Federal Aviation Administration, and the U.S. Coast Guard. For example, those in the trucking industry, aviation, or mass transit, as well as those who contract with the Department of Defense or NASA, may be required to test at least some employees for alcohol and drug use.

So if it's not usually required, why do employers drug test? Here are a few reasons:

1. To qualify for workers' compensation discounts: Many states offer employees a discount on their workers' compensation insurance premiums if they take certain steps to maintain a drug-free workplace, which may include testing job applicants.

2. To avoid liability. If an intoxicated employee harms someone on the job, the employer could be legally liable for those injuries. Workplace drug and alcohol use may also violate OSHA and sate occupational safety laws.

3. To maintain productivity and save money. According to the federal government, drug and alcohol use take a toll on the American workplace. Problems relating to drug and alcohol abuse cost $80 billion in lost productivity in a single year. Employees who use drugs are three times more likely to be late to work, more than three-and-a-half times more likely to be involved in a workplace accident and five times more likely to file a workers' compensation claim.

LEGAL LIMITS ON DRUG TESTING

Courts and legislators have recognized that drug testing implicates privacy rights. These tests don't just reveal current drug use-that is, intoxication when the test is taken. They also show past drug use, including use of legal drugs and use of drugs on the employee's own time. And, the test procedures requires the test taker to surrender bodily fluids, sometime under close supervision. Because drug testing is intrusive, state and federal laws put some limits on when, how, and whether it can be done. Generally, current employees have greater rights in the area than applicants, because employees already hold a job that they stand to lose if the test comes back positive; applicants stand to lose only an opportunity to get a job. Prospective employers can't force you to take a drug test. However, they can generally require you to take one as a condition of employment, as long as they follow the rules. If you don't want to take the test, you can take yourself out of the running for the job.

Here are some of the legal limits that might apply to applicant drug testing:

1. Disability discrimination claims.

An applicant who is taking medication for a disability is protected from discrimination by the American with Disabilities Act(ADA). Some prescribed medications turn up on drug test and some drugs that would otherwise be illegal (such as opiates) are legitimately prescribed for certain conditions. If an applicant is turned down because of a positive drug test, and the applicant's medication was legally prescribed for a disability, the company could be liable.

2. Other discrimination claims. If a company singles out certain groups of applicants- for example by race or disability- for drug testing, it could face a discrimination claim. If testing is allowed, it may be fine for the employer to single out certain job classifications for testing (for example, those that are safety-sensitive), but the employer should test all applicants for those positions.

3. Violation of state-required procedures. Although virtually all states allow applicant drug testing, many states impose procedural and other requirements. For example, some states allow drug test only after the applicant has received an offer of employment conditioned on passing the test. A number of states require employers that test to provide written notice or indicate in their job postings that testing is required.

Job Offer Checklist

☐ Job Content

☐ Salary

☐ Benefits

☐ Hours / Schedule

☐ Location

☐ Work Environment

☐ Company Culture

☐ Growth

☐ Travel

Chapter 7

EVALUATING A JOB OFFER

• •

In This Chapter You Will Learn

   ➢   How to evaluate a job offer.

• •

When you received a job offer, you must decide if you want the job or not. Fortunately, most companies will give you a few days to accept or reject an offer. There are many issues to consider when assessing a job offer. Consider the company as a whole and also the entire compensation package-salary, benefits, perks, work conditions- not just the paycheck. Weigh your pros and cons and take some time to mull over your offer.

THE COMPANY

Getting background information on the company can help you to decide whether it is a good place for you to work. Factors to consider include the company's business or activities, financial condition, size, age, and location.

THE JOB

Even if everything else about the job is attractive, you will be unhappy if you dislike the day-to-day work. Determining in advance whether you will like the work may be difficult. However, the more you find out about the job before accepting or rejecting the offer, the more likely you are to make the right choice.

MONEY

Money isn't the only consideration, but, it is an important one. Is the offer what you expected? If not, is it a salary you can accept without feeling insulted? Will you be able to pay your bills? If your answer is no, then don't accept the offer, at least right away. Make sure that you are getting paid what you're worth and you are happy with the compensation. Nobody wants to be in a position where they realize that the salary isn't enough-after they have accepted the job offer. If the compensation package isn't what you expected, consider

negotiating salary with your future employer.

BENEFITS AND PERKS

In addition to salary, review the benefits and perks offered.

Sometimes, the benefits package can be as important as what you get

in your paycheck. If you're not sure about the benefits that are offered,

ask for additional information or clarification. Find out details on

health and life insurance coverage, vacation, sick time, disability, and

other benefit programs. Inquire about how much of the benefits costs

are provided by the company, in full, and how much you are expected

to contribute. If there are a variety of options available, request copies

of the plan descriptions so you can compare benefit packages.

HOURS AND TRAVEL

Before accepting a job, be sure that you are clear on the hours and

schedule you need to work. Also, confirm what, if any, travel is

involved. If the position requires 45 to 50 hours of work a week and

you're used to working 36 hours, consider whether you will have difficulty committing to the schedule. If the nature of the job requires that you will need to be on the road three days a week, be sure that you can commit to that, as well. Also, consider travel time to and from work. Is the commute going to take an extra hour or will there be parking fees you're not paying now?

FLEXIBILITY AND COMPANY CULTURE

Many of us, with small children or elderly parents, or other personal considerations, need flexibility in our schedules. To some of us, the ability to work a schedule that isn't a typical forty hour in the office work week, is important.. It is also important to feel comfortable in the environment that you are going to be working in. One candidate for a customer service job realized that there was no way she could accept it, despite the decent salary, when she was told she had to ask permission to use the restroom. Ask if you can spend some time in the office, talking to potential co-workers and supervisors, if you're not sure that the work environment and culture are a good fit.

YOUR PERSONAL CIRCUMSTANCES

The bottom line in accepting a job offer is that there really isn't one. Everyone has a different set of personal circumstances. What might be the perfect job for you could be an awful job for someone else. Take the time to review the pros and cons. Making a list is always helpful. Also, listen to your gut-if it's telling you not to take the job, there just might be something there. Keep in mind, that if this isn't the right job for you, it's not the end of the world. The next offer might just be that perfect match. It's much easier to turn down an offer than it is to leave a job that you have already started. The employer would prefer that you decline, rather than having to start over the hiring process a couple of weeks down the road if you don't work out. So, do take the time to thoroughly evaluate the offer. Ask questions, if you have them. Take the time you need to make an educated and informed decision so you feel as sure as possible that you and the company have made an excellent match.

Chapter 8

NEGOTIATE SALARY AND

BENEFITS

• •

In This Chapter You Will Learn

> ➤ Tips on negotiating salary and benefits.

• •

When attempting to negotiate salary and benefits with an employer, you should be aware that it is a delicate situation. If you back off too quickly, you could lose out on more or better benefits; however, if you push the issue too far, you'll wind up without a job at all.

When interviewing for a new job, your prospective employer should already know the salary and benefits you are requesting. Most professionals put salary objectives on their resume while others prefer to discuss it in person; either way, the sooner the employer knows your bottom line, the better. There is no reason to waste your time or the employer's when your salary and benefits requirements aren't compatible. Further, you will establish early on that you have an objective, which will give the employer a heads-up that you plan to negotiate the first offer.

You shouldn't enter into salary and benefits negotiations with the mindset that you are doing battle with an adversary. Instead, approach it from a mutually beneficial standpoint; higher salary and better benefits equal a more productive employee. Never make demands or issue ultimatums, because not only is it counter-productive, but employers will not waste time with someone they don't consider a team player. If you notice that the employer is getting peeved, back off right away. You'll have to use communication and interpersonal skills to gauge your progress.

LOOK AT THE BIG PICTURE

It is rare for an employee to be offered both salary and benefits commensurate with what he or she desires. Something will have to give, so you should be sure to look at the big picture. For example, let's say that an employer's final offer is 10% lower than your objective. Right off the bat, you might not be interested in the offer because it is significantly lower than what you desire. However, analyze other aspects of the job. For example, is there an employee evaluation in six months? If so, you could easily close that 10% gap just six short months into your employment. Things like that should have bearing on your final decision.

GIVE THE EMPLOYER A REASON

If you are attempting to negotiate salary and benefits after you've already started work--for example, one year later--your negotiation platform is slightly different. At that point, you have had an opportunity to demonstrate your skills in the position for which you have hired, which may or may not give you a bargaining chip. Evaluate your strengths and weaknesses and document the progressive, positive changes you have made. If the number of employees under your command has increased, this is a significant negotiation benefit. If you can give your employer hard data that shows you have been a major asset to the company, you'll be more likely to obtain a raise. Further, you shouldn't assume that your employer has notices everything that you have done. He or she oversees a large group of people

GET IT IN WRITING

If you have been offered a higher salary or better benefits, make sure to get that promise on paper right next to your employer's signature. As I've mentioned before, employers have a lot on their plate, and they may not remember making such a promise. Others are unscrupulous and may try to back out a few weeks down the road. As soon as you have been promised something concerning compensation, have your employer draft an agreement.

FREELANCING
IS A
SERIOUS BUSINESS

Chapter 9

FREELANCING

In This Chapter You Will Learn

> ➤ Reasons for freelancing
>
> ➤ The kind of work freelancers do.
>
> ➤ Finding work as a freelancer.
>
> ➤ Advantages and disadvantages of freelancing.

· ·

With the dismal state of today's job market and economy, most people

are looking for ways to make more money, and many are curious

about freelance work. Finding a decent job these days is not easy, and

most people can't afford to sit around waiting for potential employers

to call. Whether you are unemployed or simply want to supplement

your already-existing income, there is a whole world of freelance

opportunities out there if you are willing to pursue them. Becoming a

freelancer is a way to work at home and be independent without needing to start an actual business. As a general rule, so long as you operate under your own name you do not need to register as a business (check your home state for any special requirements). This makes it possible to get started as a freelancer overnight without a lot of hassle and with the least amount of expense.

WHAT IS A FREELANCER?

A freelancer is someone who offers services for a fee. In general terms, a freelancer works independently with no expectation of a permanent or long-term relationship with a single employer.

WHY WOULD YOU WANT TO FREELANCE?

If you suddenly get laid off, you'll need to do something in order to keep an income stream coming in. The sooner you can do that, the less financial trouble you'll be in. While you can look and look for jobs and hope you get hired, you could decide to freelance on day one and try to find work independently. If you've had an urge to be your own boss anyway, becoming a freelancer may be a good way to do it. You can even continue your job search while you freelance. Others reasons for freelancing are:

- ❖ To work less hours
- ❖ To make more money
- ❖ To have greater freedom
- ❖ To avoid stress
- ❖ To have more fun

Whatever your reason, if you're cut out for working for yourself it can be real fun, exciting and profitable. Of course, you may or may not realize the benefits you set out to gain, but you may enjoy others you never expected.

WHAT KIND OF WORK DO FREELANCERS DO?

Freelancers can be asked to do just about any kind of work you might imagine. Here are just a few of the most popular types of freelance services:

- ❖ Freelance Writer- Write books, plays, and short stories. Also both large and small companies use freelance writers to write speeches, video scripts, technical manuals and more. Web writing is also an option.

❖ Freelance Bookkeeper- Businesses used bookkeepers to set up a system of maintaining their accounts, sending out invoices, taking care of payroll, and tax issues.

❖ Freelance Photographer- Most all of the photographer are freelancers. They are hired for particular photo shoot such as wedding, parties and school day pictures. They come to the location and provide the camera, lighting and whatever other equipment that is necessary.

❖ Freelance Interior Designer- Work to help others design their work or home spaces.

❖ Freelance Event Planner- Plan corporate meeting, community events and parties.

❖ Freelance House Cleaner- Goes out to other people houses to clean.

❖ Freelance Website Designer- This field is wide opening right now. Everybody wants their own site on the internet and it takes a certain knowledge to create one. You can do this from home with your computer.

❖ Freelance Tax Practitioner- Prepare tax returns and give advice on tax matters.

❖ Freelance Landscaper- Work to improve others lawns and gardens.

❖ Freelance Computer Programmer- Can write computer programs from home or can work on-site as a contract employee.

Basically, anything you might consider doing in your own business, you can do on a freelance basis under your own name. In most cases, even in those professions where a license is required freelancing is possible.

WHAT DO YOU NEED TO FREELANCE?

To freelance, you basically just need to have something of value you can offer to potential clients. Most people draw on their employment experience and offer freelance services in areas in which they are especially talented. The following items are also useful for those who want to freelance:

- ❖ A website to promote yourself
- ❖ A dedicated business phone or cell phone number on which prospects can reach you
- ❖ A business card
- ❖ A business address (such as a post office box or mail box service)
- ❖ A portfolio of your best work
- ❖ A few references

HOW DO YOU FIND FREELANCE WORK?

The answer partly depends on the type of freelance work you want to do. But here a few freelance resources you might consider:

- ❖ Craig's List-www.craigslist.org
- ❖ Guru-www.guru.com
- ❖ V-Worker(formerly Rent-a-Coder)-www.vworker.com
- ❖ ELance-www.elance.com

E-lancing is a new twist on the idea of online auctions-and your services are on the block. E-lancing means using the Internet to post information about your skills and your fees and competing with other freelancers for work. You bid on projects or let potential employers contact you if your skills match their needs. Some Web sites charge a nominal fee to the freelancer, but most charge a fee only to the employer.

If you're just starting out, e-lancing may be the quickest (and least painful) way to land jobs. You may even end up working on a team with other freelancers your electronic employer has brought together to tackle a big project.

E-lancing jobs are available in many fields, from accounting to legal services to photography to Web design. Go to an Internet search site or job site and search on the name of your field.

Other Way of Finding Work

Although freelancing websites are a great way to find jobs, especially when you are first starting out, they are not the only way. One of the most important tactics for being successful in any business endeavor is making interpersonal connections. If you do good work and maintain strong relationships with your clients, opportunities will have a way of finding you. People and companies are always more comfortable hiring or recommending someone when they know the quality of work they can expect. One of the greatest things about freelance work is the variety of the connections you make and the work you do.

SKILLS THAT FREELANCERS REQUIRES

There are many types of people who become a freelancer. But there are certain personality traits that help make the job easier. If you hall all these traits, you might make a great freelancer. But even if you don't, you can learn some of them or figure out ways to deal with them.

When I look at successful freelancers, I see some similar skills. Here are the ones I thank are essential:

❖ Freelance are often Introverts

When I say introvert, I don't mean the stereotypical introvert who's afraid of other people. Freelancers are often people who enjoy being by themselves. They do their best work alone or in a small group. This is important because the life of a freelancer, especially at first, is often very lonely. Unless you are lucky enough to have a partner, chances are you'll spend a lot of time alone at your computer. If you would rather be chatting with your friends over the water cooler, you might not like to be a freelancer.

❖ Freelancers Must Have Good Communication Skills

While you might prefer to work alone as an introvert, to be a good freelancer you must be able to communicate well with other people. The best freelancers will have both strong written and verbal skills.

❖ Freelancers Are Ambitious

It doesn't make sense to become a freelancer if your plan is to be mediocre, and you'll have a hard time finding clients as well. Most freelancers think big and set goals to achieve what they envision.

❖ Freelancers Must Be Self-Motivated with a Strong Work Ethic

When you set off on your own, you won't have a boss sitting over your shoulder telling you "get to work." But the best freelancers don't need that because they say that to themselves. In fact, many of the freelancers I know tend to find it more difficult to switch out of work mode than their corporate counterparts.

❖ Freelancers Are Courageous and Self-Confident

In order to become a freelancer, you will inevitably meet naysayers. There will be people who assume that since you work from home you aren't actually working. Others will ask you "but what do you do for money?" or make other disparaging remarks about your ability to make a career of your freelancing. So in order to do it, you need to have enough courage and faith in yourself to believe you can do it.

❖ Freelancers Are Multi-Taskers

You have to be focused on the details and make sure that all the details are correct to be a good freelancer. There isn't an accounting department, a marketing department, and a sales department to handle those aspects of your business. You need to do them or hire them out and make sure they get done well.

❖ Freelancers Must Be Well Organized

I don't care what system you use, whether it's notches on the desk or a full-blown task management system, the best freelancers have a system that makes sure they get done what they need to get done and when.

❖ Freelancers Aren't Afraid to Plan

Planning your business as well as the sites you build as a freelancer will make you a better freelancer. Good freelancers plan for the future with an emergency fund and they plan the sites they build with design briefs.

❖ Freelancers are Professional

As a freelancer, you are the only representative of your company. Being a professional and acting professional gets you more clients and business.

❖ Freelancers Have Support Networks

The best freelancers have support networks of friends and family. You need people you can talk to when times are going well and when they are rough.

REASONS WHY YOU SHOULD NOT BECOME A FREELANCER

There are certain traits required of a freelancer for him or her to become successful at what they do, and let me be the first to tell you, freelancing is not easy. Yes, ultimately you'll end up with more freedom and spare time on your hands, but until you've mastered the art of efficiently and time management, you'll have a lot of sleepless nights and manic weekends full of work.

Therefore, YOU should NOT become a freelancer because:

❖ You're Lazy

If you don't have the drive to work and be productive when employed, what hope do you have when you don't have someone watching over you all the time, making sure you're on schedule? Freelancing requires you to have passion and energy about your field of work; that's what makes you want to get up in the morning and get to work. If you keep your bad habits whilst freelancing, it can prove to be very detrimental.

❖ You're Not Disciplined

Discipline is an extremely important trait that any freelancer needs. Discipline in the sense that you can produce a schedule and stick to it. In the end, we all procrastinate and delay to some extent, but if you don't have self-control and discipline to minimize your unproductive, wasted time, forget about freelancing. A time-wasting, unproductive freelancer is an unsuccessful freelancer. If you're going to end up spending hours upon hours longer producing a piece of work due to laziness, then what's the point of becoming a freelancer in the first place? You're meant to be saving time that you can spend on things that matter more.

❖ You're Not Interested

Whether or not you perform to a high degree when it comes to work is solely down to one thing, you interest in the field. A person can't be enthusiastic about their work if they don't have a deep interest which emanates outside of their freelance work. You can usually identify if you have a deep interest in a topic or field by looking at your hobbies. If your hobbies identify with your desire field of freelancing, that's a very positive sign.

The decision to become a freelancer is not a light one to be made. It requires long, hard thought as your career, family and way of life us at stake. Only proceed if you know you can be a success, not if you think you can.

ADVANTAGES OF FREELANCING

Freelance work offers tremendous advantages and can represent an attractive alternative to a traditional job. If you are considering a freelance career, you should explore the benefits and pitfall of freelancing. Below are 20 advantages of freelance work.

1. Flexibility of hours

Working from home or from a remote workplace as a freelancer allows you to dictate your own hours and work at times most convenient to you. Freelancers with young children, for instance, can work after the children are sleeping; freelancers with traditional employment or part-time jobs can perform their freelance work around their regular work hours. You can work when you are most productive or load up on work now to have some "me" time later.

2. Building an asset

Owning and operating a successful freelance business allows you to create an asset than may be saleable down the road. Your efforts may be rewarded not only through the present income you generate. Your reputation, client list and other business assets can net your additional income if you sell your successful business to another.

3. Work load control

As a freelance worker, you can control your work load. While clients demands can, at times, dictate your schedule, you can turn away work during busy times or accept more work during lean times.

4. Autonomy

Freelancers are highly autonomous. As business owners, they generally answer to no one (other than their clients) and operate on their own terms, at their own hours and at the rates they establish.

5. Quality of work

In some cases, particularly for freelance paralegals or new law school grads, work as a freelancer may be more fulfilling than the work assigned by a law firm or corporation. For example, new law grads in large law firms often perform monotonous tasks such as document review while freelance attorney may gain more challenging assignments such as court appearances.

6. National exposure

Freelancers are not geographically confined or limited to serving local clients; you can work for clients from across the country or across the globe. This national exposure can open doors to new clients and new opportunities.

7. New skills

As a freelancer, you will learn new skills out of necessity that you might not gain as a traditional legal employee. These skills may include marketing, sales, office management and client development as well as knowledge in a broad range of practice areas.

8. No office politics

Office politics are non-existent for solo freelancers. If you work alone, you are guaranteed to have the corner office. You are not required to attend time-wasting meetings or cut through bureaucratic red tape to gain the tools you need to do the job.

9. No commute

Working from home eliminates the daily commute to and from the office, saving your hours in travel time and the expenses of parking, fuel and car maintenance. Even if you work from a remote office away from the home, you can choose a location that is convenient and close to home.

10. Freedom

As a freelancer, you can choose the clients you wish to work with and the projects on which you work, particularly if you have excess of work. You can drop high maintenance of slow-paying clients or turn down undesirable projects if you desire.

11. Income control

Your income is the direct result of your own efforts rather than being set by the company. In most cases, the harder you work, the greater the reward.

12. Work-life balance

Because they work from home, freelancers often have a better work-life balance. You can spend more time with the children of the dog and steal moments to relax and do things you love.

13. Respect

Achieving success as a business owner adds an additional layer of accomplishment and respect to your title.

14. Tax benefits

Working as a freelancer from a home office can provide certain tax benefits including write-offs for your home office space, equipment and other business costs.

15. New opportunities

Freelancing can open doors to new clients, new skills, and new friends.

16. Casual attire

When you work from home and don't meet with clients personally, there is no need to dress up.

17. Free parking

Parking costs in some major cities can take a chuck out of your paycheck. Working from home eliminates parking expenses.

18. Diversification

Since most freelancers work for multiple clients, losing one client does not mean unemployment.

19. Full credit

When you work as a freelancer, you receive full credit for your work. You don't have to worry about the blunders of other employees, compromising your work product for the sake of the team or others taking credit for your work.

20. New connections

Freelancing will inevitably bring you into contact with new people including new clients, mentors, business associates and others.

DISADVANTAGE OF FREELANCING

The benefits of freelancing are many; better work-life balance, the ability to choose your work hours and clients and unlimited income potential. However, launching a freelance or virtual business requires careful planning and preparation. Before you make the transition from full-time employee to freelancer, you should be aware of the pitfalls of self-employment. Below are 10 drawbacks to consider;

1. Lack of Benefits

As an independent contractor, you do not receive employer-provided benefits such as vacation pay, health insurance, 401k and other common perks. Sick time is non-existent.

2. Variable Workloads

As a freelancer, you will encounter busy times and lean times. You must learn to manage workloads and balance multiple competing priorities and deadlines.

3. Variable Income

Your workload and income may vary from month to month and can be difficult to predict, particularly in the early stages of your business. Large swings in income can make budgeting difficult.

4. Round the Clock Coverage

Today's clients expect 24/7 services. You may receive client calls late at night, on weekends and while you are on vacation. As a freelancer, you must ensure that you can provide round-the-clock coverage, especially if you serve clients in other time zones.

5. Long Hours

As a new business owner, you may initially work more hours than you worked in a traditional office setting.

6. Initial Cash Investment

Most new businesses require an initial cash investment to purchase computer software, office equipment, office supplies, insurance and other business supplies. Marketing expenses, web expenses and other start-up costs can require thousands in upfront cash.

7. Lack of Job Security

Statistics show that most new businesses fail within the first two year. Moreover, you will not qualify for unemployment if your business does not succeed. For job security in the early stages of freelancing, you may want to keep your regular job and launch your freelance business part-time on the side until you develop an established client base.

8. Lack of Paid Vacation or Personal Time OFF

If you are self-employed, paid sick time or vacation time is non-existent. You must develop a back-up plan for times when you are unavailable to serve your clients or meet deadlines due to sickness, personal emergencies or vacations.

9. Lack of Bonuses

As a freelancer, you do not receive bonuses, awards or employer recognition.

10. Distractions

Working from home can pose many distractions from personal telephone calls to children, family and visitors to the lure of the refrigerator, television, household chores and personal errands. You must be focused, motivated and disciplined.

IS FREELANCING REALLY FOR ME?

The first few days of freelancing may be totally invigorating as you get settled in your new digs and start cranking up your marketing efforts. Somewhere along the way, though, you may wake up one morning and ask yourself why you ever thought you could be a freelancer. It could be one on those days when no checks are in the mail and no appointments are on the horizon, or it could be the morning after seven 16-hour killer days in a row, with no end in sight. Either way, planning your move can help you anticipate and cope with those times more easily.

Being a freelancer is like having a baby. It hurts a lot at the time, but most people forget the pain. Hang in there, and one day you'll have a beautiful offspring: your very own business.

Appendix A

GLOSSARY OF JOB SEARCH TERMS

Application

How job seekers express initial interest in working for a company; require information such as education and job history.

Aptitude

A person's natural talents.

Career

Is the pattern of work and work-related activities that develops throughout a lifetime.

Career Objective

Tell a prospective employer the type of work you are currently pursuing.

Chronological Resume

A style of resume that lists your experience and education on chronological order.

Combination resume

A style of resume that combines the best features of the functional and chronological styles by emphasizing your abilities while including a full job history.

Cover Letter

Is a letter of introduction that states the reason you're writing to an employer.

Education

The name of each school, the school address, the program you participated in, the dates you attended the school, the diploma or degree you obtained, and the course you completed.

E-lancing

Means using the internet to post information about skills and your fees and competing with other freelancers for work.

Employment

The name of each company you worked for, the dates you worked there, your job title, and your responsibilities and duties.

Freelancer

A person who sells services without working on a regular basis for any single employer.

Functional Resume

A style of resume where the experience isn't listed in chronological order, but is instead broken down by skills.

Honors

Any honors you make have obtained

Interview

A formal meeting in which a person question or evaluate another.

Job

A piece of work done as part of one's occupation or for a price.

Memberships

Any organizations that you belong to.

Networking

Involves using the vast number of people that you know-- your family, friends, neighbors, colleagues, customers, vendors, associates, etc.; as information sources for a job lead.

Personal brand

Is how we market ourselves to others. It is your professional reputation and it is defined by your goals and accomplishments.

References

People who the employer makes contact with to learn more about you.

Resume

A document that briefly describe an applicant work experience, education and interest.

Self-Appraisal

Is the opportunity to reflect on the things you did well and the things you didn't do so well.

Skills

Something that you are good at doing, it could come naturally to you or be something you have learn through experience or training.

Talent

A special creative natural ability.

Transferable skills

These are skills in one particular work environment that you can take with you from on employer to another.

Appendix B

FREQUENTLY ASKED JOB SEARCH QUESTIONS & ANSWERS

1. How long should I make my cover letter and/or resume?

Your cover letter should be no more than one page in length. It should explain who you are and why you're the best candidate for the job. It needs to be very concise, yet keep the hiring manager wanting to learn more. If you go any longer than a page, the person reading it will get bored. Your resume should also be limited to one page, especially if you've been in the workforce for a short amount of time. Hiring managers spend only 6 seconds looking through your resume, so it's important to keep it to one page filled with strong keywords to stand out.

2. What are the most important things to include in my resume?

Some essential things to include in your resume are: your name, contact information, education history, work or internship experience, and related skills. All of these details should be tailored for each individual job application. Additionally, you can include professional organizations and special awards if you think they're relevant.

3. Should I apply for a job even if I don't have the specified experience?

Absolutely! If you think you can handle the job requirements, it never hurts to apply for the position. Whether you have less years of experience than they're asking, or you are missing one of the hard skills mentioned, these don't necessarily rule you out from landing the job. Skills can be learned on the job, and if you're the best candidate, years of experience won't matter in the end. Just don't lie and say you have the qualifications when you don't.

4. How should I address a hiring manager whose name I can't find?

Sometimes the name of the hiring manager won't be listed on the job description. If it's a small company, you might be able to find a name on their website or through a quick Google search. But if after searching you still can't find the name, you should begin your cover letter: "Dear Hiring Manager."

5. How long should you wait before the following up?

If you don't hear back from an interviewer right away, don't follow up again until after the interview's deadline has passed. If the date passes and you still haven't heard anything, send a brief follow-up to remind the interviewer about your qualifications and interest in the open job. After that follow-up, you can follow-up again every 7-10 days up to two more times for a total of three follow-ups. If you still haven't heard back, you should move on.

6. Should I write a thank you letter by hand or in an email?

This is a personal preference. Actually, either one works, 89 percent of hiring managers are fine with an email note, or half of them actually prefer it. Just be sure to personalize the note. Remind your interviewer who you are, how much you want the job, and why you're the best person for it.

7. What exactly is a personal brand and why do I need one?

A personal brand is how we market ourselves to others. It is your professional reputation and it is defined by your goals and accomplishments. During the job search, you need to take charge of your own personal brand because it affects how employers see you. In a job market where everything takes places online, your reputation is especially important for landing a job.

8. Where is the best place to find a job?

There are lots of options for finding a job, and one is not necessarily better than the others. You can find jobs on mass job boards like Monster, Glassdoor and Indeed, or smaller, niche job boards specific to your profession. You can go directly to the company's website or social media. Additionally, 44 percent of new hires are made from employee referrals. It's important to utilize all of these methods to find the most job opportunities.

9. Should I use a functional resume?

Functional resumes present a number of problems to the potential employer. They often don't give all the information needed to make a decision. They have a reputation as a resume style used by applicant who have "sketchy" backgrounds (periods of unemployment, underemployment, relevant skills that haven't been utilized recently, etc.), and potential employers know this.

10. Should I list references on my resume?

No. Prepare a separate reference sheet to provide at the interview. Use the same letterhead style used on your resume and print it on matching stationary.

Appendix C

SAMPLE CORRESPONDENCE

COVER LETTER SAMPLE

Michael White
957 Cinnibar Street SE
Salem, OR 10292
(006) 600-6776
mwhite @ email . com

January 27, 2014

Mr. Donald Young
Retail Manager
K-Mart
36 SE Pelton Ct
Salem, OR 66353

Dear Mr. Young:

I would like to be considered for the position of a Retail Customer Service Representative at K-Mart, as advertised in the Daily Classifieds. Utilizing my exceptional customer service skills and demonstrated product knowledge, I would be able to contribute significantly to your bottom line.

As indicated in the enclosed resume, I strive to create continuing customer relationships to increase sales and profitability. Particularly, I am adept at:

✔ Answering to customers in a prompt and courteous manner
✔ Providing quotations and pricing information to customers
✔ Performing indoor and outside marketing activities to boost sales
✔ Managing complaints
✔ Conducting customer follow-up calls
✔ Handling cash drawer and payments

My ability to motivate fellow team members and capability of inspiring stakeholders has been commended many times by superiors. Above all, I have a demonstrated ability to work under stress for long periods of time especially during holidays.

I am looking forward to seeing you at the interview at the time of your convenience. In order to confirm the delivery of my application, I'll contact your office after two weeks. Please feel free to call me at (006) 600-6776 if any additional information will be required.

Thank you for your time and I anticipate meeting with you soon!
Sincerely yours,

(Signature)
Michael White

JOB SEARCH LETTER SAMPLE 1

Title
Company Name
Address
City, State, Zip Code

Dear Contact Person:

I'm writing to express my interest in the Web Content Specialist position listed on Monster.com. I have experience building large, consumer-focused health-based content sites. While much of my experience has been in the business world, I understand the social value of the non-profit sector and my business experience will be an asset to your organization.

My responsibilities included the development and management of the site's editorial voice and style, the editorial calendar, and the daily content programming and production of the web site. I worked closely with health care professionals and medical editors to help them provide the best possible information to a consumer audience of patients. In addition, I helped physicians learn to utilize their medical content to write user-friendly, readily comprehensible text.

Experience has taught me how to build strong relationships with all departments at an organization. I have the ability to work within a team as well as cross-team. I can work with web engineers to resolve technical issues and implement technical enhancements, work with the development department to implement design and functional enhancements, and monitor site statistics and conduct search engine optimization.

Thank you for your consideration.

Signature
first name last name

JOB SEARCH LETTER SAMPLE 2

john.donaldson@emailexample.com

Date

George Gilhooley
XYZ Company
87 Delaware Road
Hatfield, CA 08065

Dear Mr. Gilhooley,

I am writing to apply for the programmer position advertised in the Times Union. As requested, I am enclosing a completed job application, my certification, my resume and three references.

The opportunity presented in this listing is very interesting, and I believe that my strong technical experience and education will make me a very competitive candidate for this position. The key strengths that I possess for success in this position include:

•I have successfully designed, developed, and supported live use applications
•I strive for continued excellence
•I provide exceptional contributions to customer service for all customers

With a BS degree in Computer Programming, I have a full understanding of the full life cycle of a software development project. I also have experience in learning and excelling at new technologies as needed.

Please see my resume for additional information on my experience.

I can be reached anytime via email at john.donaldson@emailexample.com or my cell phone, 909-555-5555.

Thank you for your time and consideration. I look forward to speaking with you about this employment opportunity.

Sincerely,

Signature (for hard copy letter)
John Donaldson

FUNCTIONAL RESUME SAMPLE

Charles Lopez
1234 Circle Drive
Minneapolis, Minnesota 55404
(612) 555-5555

OBJECTIVE

Dependable, enthusiastic worker with more than 10 years of experience seeking a Welding or Building Maintenance position. Self-starter, dedicated to achieving high-quality results.

SUMMARY OF QUALIFICATIONS

Welding—

Developed extensive experience in a wide variety of welding styles and positions including:

MIG	TIG	ARC	Heliarc
Oxyacetylene	Air ARC	Cutting & Gouging	Automatic Seam
Plasma Cutting	Underwater	Water Cooled	Spot Welding

Fabrication— Skilled in layout and design of sheet metal and pipe. Developed extensive knowledge of sheet rollers and brakes. Followed Manufacturer's Operating Processes (MOP) to detail.

Equipment Operator— Experienced forklift operator on various sized and styles of forklifts. Skilled in the use of a variety of power tools and metal fabrication equipment including: drills, drill press, edge planer, end mill, benders, power saws, sanders, and grinders.

Equipment Maintenance— Performed general maintenance on welding equipment and production machinery. Maintained high production levels through onsite machine repairs and preventive maintenance.

Building Maintenance— Acquired experience in general construction including basic electrical repairs, carpentry, concrete, glass, spray and roller painting, plumbing, patching, and sheetrock.

SUMMARY OF EXPERIENCE

Lead Welder

- Maintained strict performance, quality, and production standards
- Trained new employees and monitored their performance during probationary period.

EDUCATION

Certificate:

Welding and Blueprint Reading

Minneapolis Community &Technical College – Minneapolis, MN

Diploma:

CHRONOLOGICAL RESUME SAMPLE

Paul Jones
6 Pine Street
Arlington, VA 12333
555.555.5555 (home)
566.486.2222 (cell)
email:phjones@vacapp.com

Experience
Key Holder, Montblanc
April 2009 - Present

- Opened new specialty boutique
- Place orders to restock merchandise and handled receiving of products
- Manage payroll, scheduling, reports, email, inventory, and maintain clientele book and records
- Integrated new register functions
- Extensive work with visual standards and merchandising high-ticket items

Sales Associate, Nordstrom - Collectors and Couture Departments
July 2007 - April 2009

- Merchandised designer women's wear
- Set-up trunk shows and attended clinics for new incoming fashion lines
- Worked with tailors and seamstresses for fittings
- Scheduled private shopping appointments with high-end customers

Bartender, Jigg's Corner
February 2005 - July 2007

- Provided customer service in fast-paced bar atmosphere
- Maintained and restocked inventory
- Administrative responsibilities included processing hour and tip information for payroll and closing register

Education
Bachelor of Arts, Ramapo College, Arlington, VA

Computer Skills

- Experience with social media and internet research

COMBINATION RESUME SAMPLE

SHIRLEY ADAMS
1234 56 th Avenue
Apartment #203
Tucson, AZ 85725
(520) 555-5555

SUMMARY
Dependable **General Office Worker** with more than 10 years of transferable experience. Proven clerical, customer service, and communication skills in a variety of settings. Upbeat, positive attitude with a history of producing quality results and satisfied customers. Computer literate.

SELECTED SKILLS
General Office
- Organized and implemented group activities in an efficient manner
- Scheduled appointments and assured timely arrival
- Maintained accurate financial records, and paid all invoices on time
- Answered phones and took accurate messages
- Prepared reports and created documents using MS Word and WordPerfect
- Located desired information using the Internet

Customer Service
- Welcomed customers and visitors in a friendly and courteous manner
- Provided customers/clients with desired information in a timely manner
- Listened, calmed, and assisted customers with concerns
- Established friendly and lasting relationships

Communication
- Utilized Internet email as an effective communication tool
- Answered phones in a courteous and professional manner
- Established rapport with diverse individuals and groups
- Demonstrated ability to express ideas in a team environment and influence action

RELATED VOLUNTEER EXPERIENCE

General Office Volunteer	Salvation Army – Tucson, AZ	5 Years
Elected Secretary	Parent Teachers Association (ISD 01) – Tucson, AZ	5 Years
Event Coordinator	Neighborhood Involvement Program Phoenix, AZ	3 Years
Group/Activities Leader	Girl Scouts of America – Phoenix, AZ	4 Years
Family Manager		

EDUCATION   GED: Maricopa County Action Self-employed – Tucson, AZ 7 Years

155

REFERENCE LIST
David Carter
123 Main Street – Woodville, TX   74350
(901) 275-6244 – dave.carter@bellsouth.net

REFERENCES

DAVID CARTER
123 Main Street- Woodville, TX 74350
(901) 275-6244-dave.carter@bellsouth.net
ALFRED JOHNSON
Teacher, William Winans High School
(601)-645-0008
a.johnson@bellsouth.net
Mr. Johnson is a former teacher and he is familiar with my computer skills and leadership ability.

REV. HENRY DUNBAR
Pastor, First Baptist Church
(601)-333-1141
revdunbar.henry@yahoo.com
Reverend Dunbar is familiar with my character and community involvement.

GLENN LINGLE
CEO- Southern Knights
(662)741-1484
glenn.lingle@yahoo.com
Mr. Lingle is a former boss who can speak on my management skills and dependability as an employee.

Appendix D

FREQUENTLY USED ACTION VERBS ON RESUMES

A
 Achieved, accomplished, adapted, addressed, analyzed, authored, authorized, assessed, assisted, appraised, amended, advised, allocated, altered, accelerated, acquired, acted, aided, assembled

B
 Budgeted, built, balanced

C
 Compiled, combined, challenged, chaired, committed, communicated, coordinated, calculated, contributed, commissioned

D
 Decided, developed, disclosed, documented, discovered, designed, determined, demonstrated, deferred, distributed, directed, devoted, drafted, doubled, diversified

E
 Exercised, expected, earned, elected, engaged, entered, engineered, employed, edited, evaluated, entertained, eliminated, exchanged, ended, exempted, endorsed, expedited, experienced, enforced, explained

F
 Facilitated, focused, financed, fueled, figured, fit, formed, fortified, functioned

G
Guided, grouped, gave, garnered, granted, generated

H
Hired, handled

I
Improved, identified, installed, inspired, interviewed, issued, invested, illustrated, implemented, incurred, innovated, inspected, invented, interpreted, instilled, inaugurated, informed, induced

J
Judged

L
Located, lectured, launched, litigated, lobbied, led

M
Mastered, managed, merchandised, modified, met, minimized, modeled, measured, moderated, motivated, multiplied, marketed, maximized, moved, mediated

N
Negotiated, noticed

O
Operated, owned, observed, oversaw, organized, obtained, oriented

P
Participated, printed, proposed, pursued, persuaded, perceived, preserved, processed, promoted, planned, performed, pioneered, passed, prioritized, provided, profiled, polled, presented, procured, purchased, placed, permitted

Q
Quoted

R
Ranked, resolved, received, rewarded, revised, revitalized, revamped, responded, restored, rejected, reinforced, reinstated, rehabilitated, remedied, redesigned, recruited, recovered, recorded, reduced, replaced, retained, retrieved, reversed, ran, raised, reached

S
Save, secured, stabilized, scheduled, screened, settled, separated, sent, selected, shaped, shortened, showed, signed, simplified, sold, staged, standardized, steered, stimulated, strategized, surveyed, supported, supplied, substantiated, supervised

T
Trained, tabulated, took, traveled, transformed, tested, transferred, tailored, targeted

U
Utilized, uncovered, united, updated, undertook, unified

V
Verified, valued, validated, visited

W
Witnessed, worked, weighed, wrote, won, welcomed

Appendix E

SAMPLE APPLICATION FOR EMPLOYMENT

Employment Application

Full Name: _____ Date:_____
Last   First   M.I.

Address: _____
Street Address   Apartment/Unit #

_____
City   State   ZIP Code

Phone: _____ Email_____

Date Available: _____ Social Security No.:_____ Desired Salary:$_____

Position Applied for: _____

	YES	NO		YES	NO
Are you a citizen of the United States?	☐	☐	If no, are you authorized to work in the U.S.?	☐	☐

Have you ever worked for this company?   YES ☐ NO ☐   If yes, when?_____

Have you ever been convicted of a felony?   YES ☐ NO ☐

If yes, explain: _____

High School: _____ Address:_____

From: _____ To:_____ Did you graduate? YES ☐ NO ☐ Diploma::_____

College: _____ Address:_____

From: _____ To:_____ Did you graduate? YES ☐ NO ☐ Degree:_____

Other: _____ Address:_____

From: _____ To:_____ Did you graduate? YES ☐ NO ☐ Degree:_____

Please list three professional references.

Full Name: _____ Relationship:_____

Company: _____ Phone:_____

Address: _____

1

Full Name: _____ Relationship:_____

Company: _____ Phone:_____

Address: _____

Full Name: _____ Relationship:_____

Company: _____ Phone:_____

Address: _____

Previous Employment

Company: _____ Phone:_____

Address: _____ Supervisor:_____

Job Title: _____ Starting Salary:$_____ Ending Salary:$_____

Responsibilities: _____

From: _____ To:_____ Reason for Leaving:_____

May we contact your previous supervisor for a reference? YES ☐ NO ☐

Company: _____ Phone:_____

Address: _____ Supervisor:_____

Job Title: _____ Starting Salary:$_____ Ending Salary:$_____

Responsibilities: _____

From: _____ To _____ Reason for Leaving:_____

May we contact your previous supervisor for a reference? YES ☐ NO ☐

Company: _____ Phone:_____

Address: _____ Supervisor:_____

Job Title: _____ Starting Salary:$_____ Ending Salary:$_____

Responsibilities: _____

From: _____ To:_____ Reason for Leaving:_____

May we contact your previous supervisor for a reference? YES ☐ NO ☐

2

163

Military Service		

Branch: _____ From: _____ To: _____

Rank at Discharge: _____ Type of Discharge: _____

If other than honorable, explain: _____

Disclaimer and Signature	

I certify that my answers are true and complete to the best of my knowledge.

If this application leads to employment, I understand that false or misleading information in my application or interview may result in my release.

Signature: _____ Date: _____

3

Appendix F

Sample Job Aptitude Test Questions

APTITUDE SAMPLE QUESTIONS

Questions 1-8
The following paragraphs are from a first year apprentice workbook.
Read the paragraphs and answer the questions.
Included in this workbook are review questions and practical assignments for each of the eight sections of this learning module. The review questions will test your knowledge and can be attempted either as homework or as the teacher directs. The answers to the questions are also included at the end of the workbook. The practical assignments will form part of each lesson and will allow you to practice what you have learnt. These assignments will also train you to use electrical measuring equipment and how to work on an electrical circuit with safety.
At the end of the module you'll be given a competency test. You need to pass all sections of the test to pass the module. If you fail any of the parts, you'll be allowed a retest, of the incomplete sections. Each test has a number of parts, in which a certain number of questions need to be answered correctly.

Aptitude Sample Questions
Questions 1 - 8
Question (1)
a) How many sections are in the learning module?
b) When will you do the practical assignments?
Answer: Will be done on the work site.
Will form part of each lesson.

Will be done at home.
Will be done when you feel like it
c) If you fail one section of the test, do you have to re sit the whole test?
Answer: No   Yes

Question (2) Order of Operations
Answer the following:

   a)$6 + 4 \times 2 =$
   b)$21 \div 7 - 4 =$
   c)$(12 + 4) \div 4 =$
   d)$(5 - 8)^2 =$
   e)$2 (10 - 4) \times 3 =$
   f)$8 + 3 \times 4 \div 2 - 1 =$

Question (3) Arithmetic
Answer

  a) i)$7 + 8 =$
     ii)$9 + 12 =$
  b) i)$18 - 7 =$
     ii)$112 - 93 =$
  c) i)$6 \times 7 =$
     ii)$11 \times 12 =$
  d) i)24 divided 8 =
     ii)72 divided 12 =
  e) i)$8^2 =$
     ii)$\sqrt{9} =$
     iii)$\sqrt{169} =$

Question (4) Percentage
  a)10% of $628 =
  b)20% of $200 =

Question (5) Estimation
An electrician is employed to wire twelve identical residential units. Each unit requires sixty-two meters of 2.5mm² cable to wire the power circuits. 2.5mm² cables sold on 100 meter drums.

Estimate how many drums of 2.5mm² cables are required to wire the power circuits in all of the units.
  Answer:

Question (6) Transposition

  Transpose the following :
  (Please use capital letters for your answers)
  a)$R_T = R_1 + R_2$
  $R_2 =$
  b)$I = \dfrac{V}{R}$
  $V =$

PYTHAGORAS' THEOREM
The following diagram is a right-angled triangle.

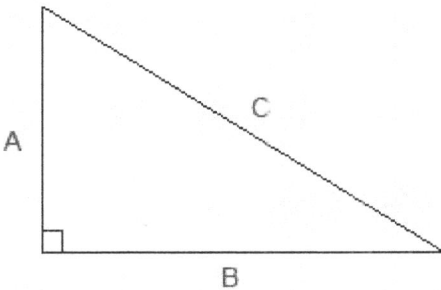

The length of the sides of the triangle can be calculated using the formula.
$C^2 = A^2 + B^2$

Question (7)

(Please round answers to the second decimal place)

a) Calculate the length of side C

Answer: C =

TRIGONOMETRIC RATIOS

The length of the sides and the angles within a right-angled triangle can be determined using trigonometry.

$$\text{Sin } \phi = \frac{\text{Opposite}}{\text{Hypotenuse}} \qquad \text{Cos } \phi = \frac{\text{Adjacent}}{\text{Hypotenuse}} \qquad \text{Tan } \phi = \frac{\text{Opposite}}{\text{Adjacent}}$$

Question (8)

a) Determine the length of the side marked Z.

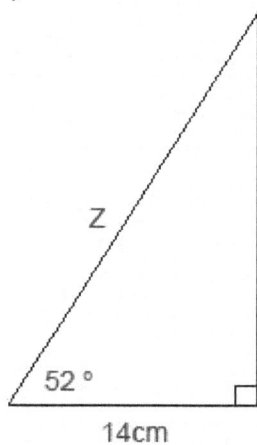

www.ingramcontent.com/pod-product-compliance
Lightning Source LLC
Chambersburg PA
CBHW071343090426
42738CB00012B/2988